In *Beyond the Lie*, Alice Smith takes you on a journey, showing how it is only when you become totally transparent as a Christian believer that you can know and walk in *total* deliverance in every area of your life. The Lord Jesus Christ is moved by each and every one of our infirmities and feelings.

Through the sacrifice of the cross that Jesus paid, every pain in our emotions can and will be totally uprooted so we can walk in and know total freedom and victory, even to the core of our being, to fulfill and accomplish our destinies on the earth.

> —Suzanne Hinn
> Co-host, *This Is Your Day*
> Benny Hinn Ministries

Alice Smith is a voice of clarity in the midst of chaos. Her clear, concise, and brilliant insights into the realm of the supernatural are revoluntionary and transformational.

> —Tamara Lowe
> Co-Founder and Executive Vice President
> Get Motivated Seminars, Inc.

ABOUT THE AUTHOR

ALICE SMITH is an internationally known conference speaker and author of the bestselling books *Beyond the Veil* and with her husband, Eddie, *Spiritual Housecleaning*. Her ministry includes teaching on intimacy in prayer, deliverance, and spiritual warfare. Alice is a regular contributor to magazines, including *Charisma, Ministries Today, Spirit-Led Woman,* and *Pray!* and makes guest appearances on the *700 Club* and *This Is Your Day*. She edits PrayerNet, an e-mail newsletter reaching thousands of praying Christians in more than 30 countries. Alice and her husband founded the U.S. Prayer Center in 1990. Alice and Eddie Smith make their home in Houston, Texas.

ALICE SMITH

Beyond the Lie

FINDING FREEDOM *from* THE PAST

BETHANYHOUSE

MINNEAPOLIS, MINNESOTA

Published by Bethany House Publishers
11400 Hampshire Avenue South
Bloomington, Minnesota 55438

Bethany House Publishers is a division of
Baker Publishing Group, Grand Rapids, Michigan.

Printed in the United States of America

ISBN-13: 978-0-7642-0176-9
ISBN-10: 0-7642-0176-X

Library of Congress Cataloging-in-Publication Data

Smith, Alice.
    Beyond the lie : finding freedom from the past / Alice Smith.
       p.   cm.
    Summary: "Brought to the feet of Christ by her own trauma, Alice Smith talks for the first time about the abuse she faced. Powerful personal testimony provides healing and help"—Provided by publisher.
       Includes bibliographical references and index.   ISBN 0-7642-0176-X (pbk.)
    1. Suffering—Religious aspects—Christianity. 2. Psychic trauma—Religious aspects—Christianity. 3. Smith, Alice, date I. Title.

    BV4909.S57   2006
    248.8'6—dc22   2005032515

DEDICATION

This book is dedicated to
my youngest daughter, Ashlee Michelle.
You are a beautiful young woman
called to complete your destiny in God.
Before you were born,
the Lord spoke to my heart from Isaiah 44:5:
"One will say, 'I belong to the LORD.'"
I pray all the days of your life
you will be known by this promise.
I love you dearly.

HOW TO CONTACT ALICE SMITH

Author, speaker, and preacher Alice Smith, and her husband, Eddie, travel worldwide to teach on various themes related to prayer, personal freedom, city strategies, and discipleship. For information about hosting Alice for a conference in your church, city, or nation, submit your online invitation at: *www.usprayercenter.org*.

Prayer Resources

Alice and Eddie Smith's books and materials, as well as other resources they recommend, can be found at: *www.prayerbookstore.com*.

Free Newsletter

Join thousands worldwide in receiving the *PrayerNet* newsletter, Alice's informative e-mail publication. Subscribe at: *www.usprayer center.org*.

To receive the Smiths' monthly *UpLink* newsletter, write to:

Alice Smith
U.S. PRAYER CENTER
7710-T Cherry Park Dr., Ste. 224
Houston, TX 77095
Phone: 713–466–4009 FAX: 713–466–5633
Toll Free in U.S: 1–800–569–4825
E-mail: usprayercenter@cs.com
Web site: *www.usprayercenter.org*
Resource Center: *www.prayerbookstore.com*

FOREWORD

You are fortunate indeed to be holding this awesome book: It could be the key that opens the door to your victorious living in the real world. Today we are constantly inundated with the message that unless our lives are perfect in every way, we're not living up to our potential. This has left many confused. Some are crushed, continually looking for life in a "demon-free zone," a trouble-free life with problem-free relationships. These people have not understood what the apostle Paul teaches in Romans 8: We live in dying bodies on a sin-cursed planet that groans as it waits for the appearance of King Jesus, adorned in resplendent glory. We all await our Messiah and the glorification of our physical bodies.

"For I consider that *the sufferings of this present time* are not worth comparing to the glory that will soon be revealed to us" (v. 18 ISV). Paul promised that God "works all things together for the good of those who love God—those who are called according to his purpose" (v. 28 ISV). He neither ran from trouble nor focused on his problems, but instead allowed pain and injustice to fashion him into the likeness of Christ. He wasn't seeking deliverance from trouble—he sought to be developed by it!

Like Paul, until Christ appears, we'll continue to experience demonic assaults and human mistreatment. The false gospels of *self-esteem, prosperity,* and *pain-free living* have done nothing but bring futility and bewilderment to those without the knowledge of Scripture.

In *Beyond the Lie,* Alice encourages us to stop beating ourselves up by expecting life on millennial-kingdom terms and realize that betrayal, victimization, and abuse will happen before Jesus ushers in eternity. It's time to get real and accept life as it is. Alice has been there, and I've seen the spiritual depth that suffering has worked into her life.

The bottom line is this: It's time for the church to acknowledge that suffering is part of God's plan for our lives. Living on this planet, under these conditions, is what the Father uses to make us like Christ.

Unless we suffer with Him, we cannot be like Him! (Romans 8:17).

Suffering isn't necessarily evidence of faithlessness or hidden sin in our lives. Until Christ returns, even the godliest among us will suffer, some more than others. Not fair? Life's not fair.

The wise will cease to complain about their suffering. They will recognize that their kingdom job assignment is sales, not management. They no longer focus on the *why* of their troubles, but on the *what.* "What is this issue producing in me for God's glory? What can this bring about in me for Christ's sake? How is the Lord using this to bring me to spiritual fruit-bearing maturity?"

Alice, my precious partner for more than three decades, is acquainted with abuse, heartache, disappointment, and betrayal. Yet she has grown to understand the place of suffering in her life—past, present, and future. As she teaches in this excellent book, suffering will either produce bitterness or "betterness." She's not allowed it to pull her down, but has chosen instead to let it build her up.

To Alice, godliness is more than commitment to Christ, it's bearing the character of Christ. Every godly person has walked the pathway of suffering. We have the privilege of fellowshipping in Christ's sufferings in order that we might be like Him. As He died *for* sin, we die *to* sin. And, like Him, we will have our Judases. Why? Because we all need a Judas to get us to our cross—the cross on which we die to sin and to self.

Beyond the Lie is more than a handbook for survival in a fallen world. Mere survival is a pathetic goal for King's kids, don't you think? Our destiny is not surviving, but overcoming! First, we must overcome ourselves, our wrong perceptions of life and living. Then, we overcome life's adversities. Finally, we overcome the kingdom of darkness.

As Alice would say, it's time to graduate from whiner to winner. This book will get you there. I hope I've whetted your appetite. There's meat inside—dig in!

—Eddie Smith

CONTENTS

INTRODUCTION

The book you are holding is the book I was never going to write. What rational person is willing to expose her inner flaws or reveal her stories of struggle, failure, and embarrassment? But the Lord has clearly shown me that the church needs the revelation I've been given. In more than thirty-five itinerant years I've counseled and ministered to thousands of people who've suffered from Satan's schemes. Like them, I've experienced this pain: I've been victimized. The question I wish to pose is this: *Why do some choose to stay in it?*

I'm weary of society's relentless venting of victimization. The nightly news has become a constant barrage of violated rights, disgruntled employees, ridiculous lawsuits, and grandstanding politicians. Someone is always whining about something. We should, and do, fight for those who've been truly maltreated, but today the whiners scream louder than those who suffer in silence.

In the 1970s, TV's *Saturday Night Live* was a cleaner comedy satire than it is today. One of their skits involved "The Whiner Family," of which members spoke with a grating, irritating whine. When they engaged in a conversation, the sounds of their voices were annoying. What made it so funny was that all of us have met constant whiners— you know, those folks who never have a positive thing to say about themselves or anyone else? One thing is for certain: *Whiners aren't winners, and winners don't whine!* This book is about winning, not whining.

Satan, our archenemy, delights in diminishing God's purpose for our lives. Forces of darkness lurk in the shadows, whispering their lies, laying in wait for opportunities to rob men and women, boys and girls, of the freedom they can have in Christ. I am furious with the devil and his demons, and I'm ready to expose them. *Beyond the Lie* will expose the lies you may have believed too.

I'm not focusing here on antidepressants, the latest counseling craze, or the buzz among psychologists and psychiatrists. Many of us have had our fill of the world's remedies. It's time the church of Jesus

Christ looks to her Savior for the answers. After all, "Everything that goes into a life of pleasing God has been miraculously given to us by getting to know, personally and intimately, the One who invited us to God" (2 Peter 1:3 THE MESSAGE). Because too few Christians know the truth of God's Word, their Christian experience is often less than the overcoming life that Scripture promises.

I've always been committed to an intimate relationship with Jesus Christ. I've known that He is my victory and has given me all manner of spiritual blessings. However, I was confused for many years, and over time I saw a recurring pattern in my life: Regardless of what I did, where I was, or how I was living, a pack of intimidating spirits tracked me like bloodhounds. Until God provided me with proper revelation, the biblical keys, and the passion to do something about it, it continued. This is why I've written *Beyond the Lie*. I'm revealing the most intimate details of my life—my story—as a testimony to God's deliverance.

Crisis is the hinge on which the door of promotion swings. Every biblical champion consistently moved from one crisis to another. How you understand, view, and deal with your crises will make or break you. It will establish your future. Your promotion is waiting, but it will not come until you choose to become the champion God has made you. As you benefit from reading my story of how I've gained victory over abuse, others can and should benefit from yours. As my late father-in-law, Dr. Robert E. Smith, taught me, "Everything God has given to me was on its way to someone else when I received it. It's my job to see that it reaches them!"

It's time *you* become "a bloodhound of heaven." It's time for you, the hunted, to become the hunter. You were created to be a champ, not a chump; a winner, not a whiner; a victor, not a victim! It's time for you to hunt down and defeat the destructive cycles in your life, saying, once for all, "Enough is enough."

CHAPTER ONE:
My Story

It's unsettling for me to share so transparently about the violation of my personal boundaries. God knows how hard this book has been for me to write, so I'm trusting Him that you will be impacted and changed by it. This is the story of my victory over victimization.

The small South Texas town where I grew up has Spanish moss drooping from the trees, winding narrow streets, and stifling humidity to which in time I became accustomed. The lazy days of summer brought us a good game of baseball, fishing at the lake, or swimming in the Gulf of Mexico. Children filled the placid streets with bikes, skates, and homemade go-carts. It was a simpler time, and our town—population 5,000—was a simpler place.

The closeness we shared as friends and family gave us a sense of security. Most everyone knew one another, so there was little need to lock our doors at night or fear walking the streets alone. Nevertheless, in the summer of 1956, I encountered a reason for insecurity: sexual abuse . . . mine.

I'm grateful for the blessing of my family, and I in no way blame my past on them. We live in a fallen world, and we should realize that parents can't protect their children from all harm (I was the youngest of four). My parents were committed to the Lord, and when the doors of our church were open, we were there. My daddy was a teacher who coached most of the public school's sports. My mother was an executive secretary for a leading chemical company.

Between basketball, cheerleading, football, and vacations, ours was an all-American family. The neighborhood kids loved to gather at our house for kickball or hide-and-seek, and Mother always had good snacks around!

THE INTRUDER

Sadly, when I was six, everything changed for me. One hot summer night I was in bed, almost asleep, when I felt a pair of hands at my waist pulling me sideways on the mattress, leaving my legs to dangle off the side. At first I was unsure of what was happening. Half asleep, I didn't know who was around at the time. My sister, who is twelve years older than I, often had guys and gals hanging out in our house; my other sister and my brother (twins) were just beginning their teenage years. But my groggy mind soon awakened as the male figure began to sexually assault me. I was stunned—I didn't know what to do—so I continued to act as if I were asleep.

My heart pounded until I feared it would beat so loud it would reveal that I was awake and aware. (Obviously, I wished I had been bold enough to speak up, but fear paralyzed me. I suspect this is a common response from small children caught in traumatic experiences.) The next ten or fifteen minutes seemed like eternity as the violation continued.

Once the shocking offense was over and he was satisfied, he turned me back into my bed. When the impact of what happened hit me, I laid trembling as tears coursed down my cheeks. The next day, and for years afterward, I couldn't bring myself to tell anyone.

What was wrong with me? How could this happen to me? Why? What did I do to deserve this? How could I make it stop? Who would believe me? Tragically, as a young girl I began to develop unfortunate preconceptions about boys and men in general. Worst of all, for many months after, my abuser continued his violation . . . and all the while I suffered in silence.

Around the beginning of the next year my sexual torment ended, but the gates of my soul were flung open to life-altering trauma and pain. My identity had changed. *I was now a victim.* Although no one knew it, like a wounded animal I instinctively hid what was happening.

THE STALKER

My chilling reality didn't end at six. When I was twelve, I experienced a different kind of victimization, this time from a stalker. Living in a small town had its privileges, like walking alone to a neighbor's house, or walking to the local theatre to watch the Three Stooges. Years had passed since I'd experienced the sexual abuse, and although it was a secret I kept until I married my husband, Eddie, the emotional scars and faulty thought patterns had already formed.

My mother went to work every day, while during the summer months Daddy worked part-time at the chemical plant. My brother and sister were in and out of our house throughout the day.

One morning Mother left for work early, and Dad departed a little later. My brother and sister were taking senior lifesaving lessons at the city pool. I was alone in the quiet house, enthralled with TV cartoons, when the phone rang. As I picked up, a mysterious man on the other end began to whisper, "I know where you live. I like you." Then he said some sexual things and laughed. Panic seized my heart as I quickly hung up. In a flash, the memories of my past abuse flooded my mind.

When this perverted narcissist called again, I screamed at him to shut up and leave me alone; with a sinister snicker he acted as if he actually enjoyed my angry response. Once more I slammed down the phone. He didn't call again that day, but I locked all the doors and felt like a prisoner inside my own home. That evening as I told my parents what had happened, they were sympathetic, but because such behavior was so unheard of in our little town, they believed it wouldn't happen again.

Now, I had always been part of our church, but I wasn't born again until age fifteen. At twelve I didn't have the power of the Holy Spirit to calm me or give me direction and courage, but after receiving Christ as my Lord and Savior, my one desire and passion was to be close to Him. I was confident that the Jesus I'd heard about in Sunday school and read about in the Bible would never deceive or abuse me. *You can be just as confident of this:* Any abuse you have suffered did not happen with God's approval. When people make choices for evil that result in harm to you, your heavenly Father grieves over your pain and makes a way for your victory.

The torment persisted off and on for a couple of weeks, resuming when the unrelenting, lust-filled man dialed again several days later. He had to be living somewhere within sight of my house, because he would call about five minutes after Daddy left for work. Near our home were several sets of rented fourplexes, and my parents learned that a single man occupied the upstairs apartment several lots down from us, though we were never sure if he was the one calling.

The conclusion came the day Daddy told me he had a strategy (I was apprehensive). He drove away, then parked his truck around the corner and ran through neighboring backyards to our house just as the phone was ringing. When he answered and heard the man's foul, demonic words, he screamed at the top of his lungs in his big coaching voice something to be feared: "Don't you ever call here again—I know who you are, and I will get you!" Then he blew his whistle as loud as he could into the phone, and we could both hear the man scream at the other end.

Daddy hung up and soothed my fears. Throughout the summer, friends and family watched over me. Though that man never called again, my self-identity as a victim was renewed—and strengthened.

THE GROPER

At seventeen I was entering adulthood, ready to put behind me the childhood traumas I'd endured. My dream was to enter the ministry, so when I was invited to sing at a youth evangelism conference near Houston, I was thrilled. Praise God, the weekend was a success, as over one hundred teens came to Christ. The evangelist, a college athlete, commanded many speaking opportunities in our state as well as throughout the nation.

On Sunday he and I were scheduled to minister at the large local church where the crusade had been held. Between the two morning services, this handsome college boy asked if I wanted to go for a ride. It was a gorgeous spring day, so without hesitation I said, "Sure."

We cheerfully talked about the souls saved that weekend and about our individual dreams for the future. He attended a reputable college, but I was still in high school. I felt honored to work in the crusade at such a young age, especially with a well-known preacher.

I hadn't noticed that while I was speaking nonstop, he had intentionally driven down a gravel road to an obvious dead end. When I realized it, my heart began to race.

I quieted and asked, "Where are we going?"

"Nowhere in particular," he replied. "I just thought we could talk better if we stopped."

My natural exuberance changed to nervous concern. After he parked the car, he talked for a few minutes . . . then tried the unimaginable. The burly, strong evangelist placed his hand on my leg and tried to move it up. I told him to stop and pushed away his hand, which must have either angered or challenged him, for now he was fighting to get his way.

However, I fought back—I would *not* go through this again. I pulled my feet up and started to kick like a wild animal, all the while screaming for him to leave me alone. He realized he had tampered with the wrong person, and with a wounded ego (at least) he straightened himself in his seat and then silently we drove back to the church, where after the second service I shared with the pastor what had happened. The pastor, who was mentoring the youth evangelist, scolded him for his reckless behavior. (*Note:* I don't know if this guy took his counsel or not. He is still in evangelism—but divorced and remarried.)

Even though I was born again and living for the Lord, I had attracted that same seducing and violating spirit. What was up with this? It was as if I had a sign around my neck: "Go ahead and abuse me." Not only was this my unfortunate introduction to Christian ministry, but it would take me many years to learn how to stop the cycle.

I should add that space won't allow me to list and describe the *honorable, holy* ministers with whom I've served over three-plus decades. They are committed to God, to their wives and families, to their churches and ministries, and they've honored me as a sister in Christ, a fellow minister of the gospel. I salute them!

THE PEEPING TOM

When I was eighteen, about to graduate from high school, I led one of the boys in my high school choir to Christ. James, who had a gorgeous, pure tenor voice, had lived through a tragic childhood: He didn't know his father, his living conditions were poor, and he suffered from self-esteem issues. Because of his talent, no one was surprised when he won the lead in the school's spring musical. This was a great boost for his confidence, and he played it for all it was worth.

I see now that I was James' mentor and role model. He sought my attention and desperately wanted me to be his girlfriend. I wasn't interested in him, other than being his friend, and this deepened the rejection he felt.

One night around two o'clock, I awakened with a start to a scratching at my window. When I pulled back the curtains, there was James with a frantic look on his face. "Come out here. I need to talk to you."

I told him to go home, that I would see him at school the next day. Infuriated, he screamed nonsensical words, then stomped around in our backyard like a madman. I began to pray for the Lord's protection over me and my family.

Instead of leaving, James began to relentlessly hurl small stones at my window. I hated to wake my parents, but I knew I must. My father went outside to have a firm and direct conversation with my confused friend, and, thank God, the rest of the night was peaceful.

Though it would be years before I would recognize the pattern of this cycle in my life and know how to stop it, thankfully, each time the adversary violated my boundaries, I gained increasing discernment. (Many who suffer abuse don't learn to establish their personal boundaries, and their problems intensify.) Don't let the unfortunate details of my past overshadow the glorious victory I've experienced in Christ! Almighty God has rescued me from the web of victimization, and I'm excited to share with you how He's done it.

This is an important key, so don't overlook it: Once the door of victimization and trauma is open in your life, it remains open until you (the victim) slam it shut. Your pastor can't close the door for you, neither can your friends, your counselor, or your spouse. *You must do it!* I've shut that door for good and removed the welcome mat. If you are to achieve victory, you also must establish the boundaries of how you will or will not allow others to treat you. In *Beyond the Lie,* you will learn how to close the gate and live in freedom.

WHY?

As parents, we know that one of the first questions toddlers ask is "Why?" When faced with injustice, *we* often ask the same of God. When I asked Him in prayer why such "junk" kept happening to me, He didn't answer me immediately and directly, but I did feel His presence and protection. This is one of the sweet passages He gave me:

> Many there be which say of my soul, There is no help for him in God.
> But thou, O LORD, art a shield around me; my glory, and the lifter up of mine head.
> I cried unto the LORD with my voice, and he heard me out of his holy hill.
> I laid me down and slept; I awaked; for the LORD sustained me.
> I will not be afraid of ten thousands of people, that have set themselves against me round about.
> Arise, O LORD; save me, O my God: for thou hast smitten all mine enemies upon the cheek bone; thou hast broken the teeth of the ungodly. (Psalm 3:2–7)

If you feel apprehensive about the process, you don't need to be! This book could unlock your future, so keep reading and take action. There's a fire in my soul right now. I feel the Lord would have me make this prophetic declaration:

God wants to move His church from a victim mentality to a victor mentality.

Like many others, you have been challenged with trials and afflictions that have left you battle-scarred and weary. Just when you think the storm is over, the enemy rushes in like a flood and overwhelms you.

Perhaps you have quietly hidden in yesterday's guilt and shame. But this is a new day and a new season. There's a shift occurring in the heavenlies, and the Lord is giving fresh revelation about truths for freedom.

Your eyes shall be opened to the fullness of what Christ's death and resurrection accomplished. You will no longer walk as a victim of circumstance; you will look your spiritual adversaries straight in the eye and speak the Word of Truth into each situation.

In His fiery crucible, God is fashioning His most dreaded warriors. You can be delivered from circumstances that have left you stripped of dignity. If your boundaries have been violated so often that you've acquired a victim mindset and accepted defeat . . . no more! Today declare that the game is over.

God is telling you to look up and rise above that mindset. You can be an overcomer—He will show you what to overcome. In order for David to be victorious, he had to confront Goliath; however, when he pursued God in total dependency, he knew God would back him up. As he slung his stone in faith, the Lord's power met it and slew the giant.

You too will face your giants. The Almighty is commanding you to release anointed stones in the power of His name. Let them fly. Your giants will fall as you step out in faith!

CHAPTER TWO:
Forms of Abuse

It's difficult to believe that anyone will live their entire life without suffering mistreatment at some point. No one is alone when it comes to struggles. Nevertheless, what *each* of us does with our hurts ultimately affects our physical and spiritual health.

While everyone hits bumps in the road of life from time to time, a person with a victim mentality will hit them on a regular basis. He or she may chalk it up to "bad luck," but there's usually much more to it than mere happenstance. Because the cycles become repetitive, the victim begins to assume abuse is normal or, worse yet, deserved. In time, he or she may even attempt to justify and protect the abusers.

The saddest cases are those involving innocent children. In the U.S. in 2002, for instance, babies less than one year old to children seventeen years of age were documented as mistreated. Neglect accounted for roughly 63 percent of the cases; physical abuse, 19 percent; sexual abuse, 10 percent; and psychological abuse, 8 percent. Recent studies in Colorado and North Carolina estimate that as many as 50 to 60 percent of deaths resulting from abuse or neglect aren't even recorded;[1] they also indicate that neglect is the most under-recorded form of fatal maltreatment.

Victimization rates decline as age increases, and rates were similar for male and female victimization, except for cases of sexual abuse, in which the rate for girls was almost four times that of boys.[2] The abuser is typically someone who'd been charged with caring for the child. And did you know that between 30 and 40 percent of all reported incest cases involve an alcoholic parent?[3]

In the United States, a rape is reported about once every five minutes.[4] Worse, rape is called "the most underreported violent crime in America." In a large national survey of women, only 16 percent of the rapes had ever been reported to the police.[5] In a study conducted by the

Department of Justice and the Centers for Disease Control and Prevention, researchers interviewing eight thousand women and eight thousand men found that one in six women had experienced an attempted or completed rape. At the time they were assaulted:

- 22 percent were under the age of twelve
- 54 percent were under the age of eighteen
- 83 percent were under the age of twenty-five[6]

From the *Rape in America* study:

- 60 percent of the women who reported being raped were under eighteen
- 29 percent were under eleven
- 32 percent were between eleven and seventeen
- 22 percent were between eighteen and twenty-four
- 7 percent were between twenty-five and twenty-nine
- 6 percent were older than twenty-nine
- For 3 percent, age was not available.[7]

Also, date rape is pandemic on America's college campuses. In the same study, 80 percent of the females raped were victimized by someone they knew.[8]

Sexual abuse isn't the only subject I'm addressing in this book— there is also domestic violence, greed, dishonor, verbal and emotional abuse, betrayal, abandonment, poverty, stalking, and many other forms of abusive behavior. Regardless of the specific issue, once we've suffered a traumatic experience, we need to diagnose what's happening. For now, let's look at some abusive situations.

Sexual Disgrace

Joey was the neighborhood's most popular kid. He was the one to start the games, inviting all his friends to play. His rural community was friendly and close.

One of the boys who joined in was a high schooler. All the other kids, including Joey, looked up to him, the witty star of the football team. The children were thrilled when he played with them.

One day, after the outdoor games, the older boy asked Joey if he wanted to see his new computer. Joey, amazed that this popular jock had invited him over, accepted. Inside his room, he had Joey sit beside him, and then flashed pornographic pictures on the PC screen, asking Joey what he thought.

Uncomfortable but curious, Joey continued to watch—he didn't want to come across as uncool. The obscene displays changed into depictions of gay activity, and before Joey realized what was happening, he lost his innocence, feeling ashamed, confused, and vulnerable. When his new "friend" suggested they play games that led to sexual promiscuity, Joey knew it was wrong, but he justified it anyway.

Now grown and in the business world, Joey fights for respect among his peers. A male colleague mysteriously sued him for sexual harassment, even though he was innocent. Associates made sport of his curly hair and shy personality, calling him a "girly boy." The final blow came when he discovered his wife was having an affair. Stunned and disgraced, Joey suffers in silence, wondering how all this started and longing to make it stop.

Betrayal

John and Joan had been happily married twenty-six years, with three beautiful children, two of whom were already on their own. John was a faithful deacon; Joan was the church children's director. They loved the Lord and freely gave their tithes and offerings. Finances had never been a problem for them, even from the beginning of their marriage.

John had been employed with the same company since college days—a small, struggling enterprise when he began. He started on the ground floor. It fulfilled his creative side, he liked the adventure, the retirement pension was extremely attractive, his peers respected him, and he'd been promoted regularly. At the rate he was going, he projected that in a year he'd be company president; the trustees, the directors, and the outgoing president, with many of whom he golfed, assured him he was the man for the job.

One day John arrived at work and heard only the peculiar hum of lowered voices. Nothing could have prepared him for the shock of walking into his partially empty office and seeing the pink slip on top of his cleared desk. Utterly confused, he went to the president's office and was told he no longer had a job. No one would talk to him. The president, a good friend for many years, wouldn't explain why—John was simply fired. He left disgraced and without answers.

Three months later John learned that his best friend, who was less qualified, had been given the presidency. He considered a lawsuit, but decided it wasn't worth the fight. John gave his best years to the company and has little to show for his faithfulness. It was a stinging betrayal; he's wounded and hurting. John never struggled with depression until now.

Overwhelming pain compelled him to step down from his deacon position and stop going to the men's prayer breakfast. The experience shook his faith in God, his self-confidence, and led to a cycle of mistrust, isolation, and bitterness. When he tries to pray, he feels empty and alone.

Torment

Stephanie always felt awkward in everything she did. She struggled with school, money, relationships, acceptance, and her appearance. She was born to a sixteen-year-old who'd had a one-night fling but didn't really want a child; Stephanie lived nine years with her frustrated mother, who constantly told her she wasn't wanted. Her deadbeat father couldn't care less about her. At nine, she moved in with her grandmother and step-grandfather, who were resentful at feeling "obligated" to rear a child.

All Stephanie wanted was to be embraced by others, and her anxiety made her accident-prone. As a child, she broke an arm while riding her bike; as a teen she broke a leg while water-skiing. The kids at school called her "Dropsy" because she was always spilling food or scattering papers. She frequently contracted various illnesses.

Stephanie landed a great job after college, one she was certain would help her future. Just when things were looking up, though, Stephanie almost lost her position because of transportation problems: When she crashed and wrecked three cars in two years, her insurance company refused to pay off the third, leaving her under a mountain of debt. In her distress she forgot to purchase insurance for her fully paid secondhand vehicle. Several months later, when she was stopped and ticketed for running a red light, she placed the ticket in her glove box and forgot about it, then was shocked when she was arrested for unpaid traffic fines. Suffering from a lifetime of rejection, without money, and with chaos seemingly surrounding her, Stephanie lost her job. She feels cursed. Dogged by a tormenting spirit, she wonders why she has so many struggles.

Injustice

Juan's parents legally immigrated from Mexico when he was very young. Years later, Mr. and Mrs. Gonzalez were realizing the American dream. Though they didn't have so much by U.S. standards, they saved their money so that Juan could go to school, get a good job, raise a family, and prosper.

Juan was a hard worker. When his friends went out, he stayed home to study, and at last his faithfulness and diligence paid off handsomely when he graduated third in his high school class of over eight hundred. Juan was the first in his close-knit family to achieve academically, and they were so proud of him . . . but his excitement turned to disappointment when he learned that he didn't get a college scholarship.

He did make it into undergraduate school through his own efforts. There he reconnected with William, a high school buddy who was studying for the same degree and had graduated eighty-ninth in the class of eight hundred. When Juan asked how he was paying for college, William replied that he'd been given a full four-year scholarship. Juan went to the admittance office repeatedly to find out why he had not qualified, but he was turned away without answers.

Abandonment

Six-year-old Ricky loved his parents, as well as his two older sisters and younger brother with whom he played every day after school on the playground. Ricky's mother, a humble, quiet woman, never worked outside the home. She married right out of high school and was pregnant within two months.

One morning Ricky heard his mother crying in the kitchen. Worried, he got out of bed to check on her. She tried to console him although she was obviously upset, and the bewildered boy knew something was terribly wrong. When Ricky and his siblings came home from school later that day, they asked where their daddy was. Mama sat them down and tearfully explained that Daddy wasn't coming back—he no longer wanted to be married or to rear his children. They burst into tears. "What are we going to do?" Ricky's twelve-year-old sister asked. "I'm not sure, honey, but we'll manage," Mama was able to say.

They barely managed. Ricky's mother took two jobs, and the children hardly saw her. She seldom smiled. The family, who'd once been comfortable, now wore secondhand clothes and hardly had enough food to eat.

Little Ricky missed his daddy and couldn't understand why he'd left them. Ricky concluded that it was his fault—after all, he didn't always put away his toys when Daddy asked. And maybe all the kids were too rowdy. Whatever the causes, Ricky never saw his daddy again.

As a young adult, Ricky found a woman to marry—*everything* he hoped to find in a girl. Soon they had two children, and life was good. About five years after their wedding, though, seemingly bizarre thoughts began to surface. Ricky felt a strong urge to leave his wife and children. He felt plagued inside, night and day. Why would he want to sabotage these wonderful relationships? He prayed for answers, talked to several friends, even asked his minister for help. Ricky loves his family, but the spirit of abandonment he experienced as a child persistently hounds him to act out in the same way.

Calamity

Ron and Betty, fine Christian influencers in their city, own a successful family business. One day a disgruntled employee, mad at Ron, set the business on fire. Ron and Betty lost everything. They spent thousands of dollars to hire an attorney to prosecute the delusional man. But their insurance policy, which hadn't been reviewed in years, wasn't sufficient, so they were forced to secure a personal loan to rebuild the business. Meanwhile, their vacation home was damaged by wind and water, and they increasingly felt as if the world were caving in on them. Their credit cards were maxed out, their savings spent. Trapped by the weight of it all, they despaired, crying out to the Lord for understanding and help.

Dishonor

Pastor James and his family had a devastating experience at his last church. The verbal abuse they suffered left them weak and tired as vicious lies circulated. Unable to deal with it all, he quietly resigned. Pastor James was never much of a fighter, for it was his nature to let others have their way. He'd led this growing congregation for over sixteen years, and members were shocked at his "sudden" choice. They knew neither the whole story nor about the political games played behind the scenes.

Predictably, the elders voted not to have a celebration for the pastor's family or to offer any financial compensation for his years of faithful service. Several members complained to the elders and staff but didn't press the matter for fear of being seen as not submitting to authority. They won their struggle for power in the church.

James decided to find secular employment until he and his family recovered from the betrayal. With his business degree, it wasn't hard to find work that fit his qualifications. His heart was to pastor, but that would have to wait.

While it was extremely challenging for them to plug into another church, eventually the family found a fine congregation to join, and they sat quietly in services for months. One year later, James went to the senior pastor and offered to serve as a Sunday school teacher, which was accepted. He was gifted, with a vast wealth of Bible knowledge, and many in the church appreciated him. His attendance was so large that the room routinely overflowed.

One Sunday afternoon the associate pastor called to tell James he needed to submit all his material to the senior pastor for approval before teaching it. No other teacher had to do this, but he had nothing to hide, so James submitted his outlines each week. A month later, he was shocked when asked to step down from teaching—someone in the class had reported to the staff that he was promoting false doctrine. Confused at the accusation, James asked to have a meeting with the offended person so the issue could be resolved. The senior pastor refused. Dishonored again, James returned weekly to sitting in a pew at another church.

Whether it's battery, betrayal, accident-proneness, dishonor, injustice, poverty, abandonment, or one of the various forms of sexual mistreatment: *Abuse is abuse.* It is a sin against the victim, but first and foremost it's a sin against God. Why? For two reasons. First, because God has created each of us in His own image. The victimized person bears God's image and was created to share His love and fulfill His purposes. Second, because God uniquely identifies with us. Jesus is acquainted with our grief. He hurts when we hurt: "Whatever you did for one of the least of these . . . you did for me" (Matthew 25:40 NIV).

Ever since Satan victimized Adam and Eve in the garden, where God had given them dominion over the earth (see Genesis 1:28), sinful people have sought to dominate others. Concurrently, synergistically, Satan and his demons have enabled and empowered man's lawless abuse against others.

The tendency of man's fallen nature is to tear down and exploit; man, left to his lower nature, leans toward manipulation and control. God never intended for man to rule man—the kingdom authority He authorized man to exercise was for the purpose of restoring, building up, and planting.

Until Jesus returns we are to live as godly influences on the earth. "The kingdom of God is within you" (Luke 17:21 NIV), so "Go ye therefore, and teach all nations, baptizing them in the name of the Father, and of the Son, and of the Holy Ghost: Teaching them to observe all things whatsoever I have commanded you: and, lo, I am with you alway" (Matthew 28:19–20).

A believer's kingdom authority is the antithesis of victimization. In victimization, evil people and demons try to damage others to keep them trapped in a cycle of despair so they will never step into their destiny. God's design is to make you a danger to the kingdom of darkness. God's way is to use us to build up, to restore, and to minister life through acts of righteousness. We are to be life-changers so that God's kingdom authority can manifest on earth as it is in heaven.

That's His plan for you. No reason to remain discouraged. Many influential men and women have suffered through traumatic situations and risen above them. If you press forward, you too can defy the hindrances that affect your destiny.

Time-management expert Ted Engstrom says:

Cripple him, and you have a Sir Walter Scott. Lock him in a prison cell, and you have a John Bunyan. Bury him in the snows of Valley Forge, and you have a George Washington. Raise him in abject poverty, and you have an Abraham Lincoln. Strike him down in infantile paralysis, and he becomes Franklin Roosevelt. Deafen him, and you have a Ludwig van Beethoven. Have him or her born black in a society filled with racial discrimination, and you have a Booker T. Washington, a Marian Anderson, a George Washington Carver. . . . Call him a slow learner, "retarded," and write him off as uneducable, and you have an Albert Einstein.[9]

CHAPTER THREE:
Emotional Responses to Abuse

Ronnie was plagued with rejection and worthlessness, constantly battling his feelings of being stupid and clumsy. The nightmare began when he was only five. Violence, rage, and fear ruled his home; he watched his parents war against each other to the point of being terrified that one would kill the other.

"Hit me, you stupid man!" his drugged mom taunted. "You're not strong enough to do it, are you?" Her enraged husband moved in close and caught himself just before following through. Little Ronnie was peeking around the door, watching the altercation.

"You're not worth it," his inebriated dad hurled back, grabbing his jacket and keys before storming out the door. Though this battle had waned, there would be more . . . many more. It was years later that Ronnie realized his parents' quarrels resulted from drug and alcohol addiction.

Ronnie was often alone at night. His father would stay at the bars until he had to come home, and his mom was so stoned she didn't know or care about Ronnie's needs. It was common for him to find his own meals at a young age.

One day ten-year-old Ronnie waited over an hour for his dad to show up and retrieve him after school. When he climbed into the car, he voiced a complaint about the wait. His drunken father was livid; after they got home he grabbed Ronnie by the collar and then beat him without mercy, shouting, "You're nothing, boy!" The words drove the wound of rejection deeper into Ronnie's mind and heart.

When Ronnie tentatively asked for food or school supplies, his mother would yell, "Why did I have you? You're nothing but trouble—I wish you were dead!" His heart felt like it was being pierced with daggers. Ronnie came to believe he was a mere inconvenience, so he repeatedly ran away from home, only to be brought back by a neighbor or the police.

In time Ronnie saw himself as a waste of humanity who should never have been born. To numb his pain, like his parents before him, he turned to chemicals. His parents didn't care—in fact, he felt that no one cared. His habit was expensive, but then a friend showed him how to steal money from girls' purses at school. The adrenaline rush from theft gave him a sense of power he'd never felt; in trouble with the law, confused and angry, Ronnie quit school and focused on stealing.

Years of destructive behavior took its toll. Jobless and without a purpose for living, Ronnie wondered why he was alive. One afternoon he saw Joshua Stanley, a neighborhood friend he'd played with as a child. Joshua was different from other kids—smart, gentle, clean-cut—and now was in his second year at the local university. As they struck up a conversation, Joshua invited Ronnie to dinner at his house that evening.

Ronnie was attracted to something about Joshua, but he didn't know what. In fact, the Stanleys are fine Christians who live their faith. Later, at the table, Mr. Stanley asked, "Ronnie, if you were to die tonight, where would you spend eternity?"

"I wish I would die—this world has nothing to offer me!" he responded sarcastically.

"Is that how you really feel, Ronnie?"

Getting honest, Ronnie said, "I don't know, Mr. Stanley. I'm all messed up."

That night Mr. Stanley shared the gospel, and Ronnie gave his life to Christ and was instantly and radically changed.

Ronnie joined their church and enrolled in a two-year discipleship program Mr. Stanley taught. Learning the Word of God and his identity in Christ opened the way for him to address the root of his rejection. "I found victory and freedom from the past," Ronnie testifies. "I broke the cycle of emotional rejection and lies by embracing God's truth about me and allowing Him to heal my broken human spirit. Then I firmly commanded the evil tormentors to leave. Once I got mad at the devil and said out loud that I wouldn't be his victim any longer, things started to change in me."

Ronnie learned to submit his emotions to the Spirit of God, who was now dwelling in his heart. He would no longer be the victim of emotional mismanagement. He was now Spirit-led, not emotion-driven.

BIBLICAL EXAMPLES

The Bible describes many instances of victimization. Let's consider three of them.

The Midianites who oppressed Gideon and his family constantly ruined their crops (Judges 6). Fearing that they'd see him, Gideon threshed wheat while hidden by a mountain and a great oak. When the angel of the Lord came to him, He announced, *"The* LORD *is with you, mighty warrior"* (v. 12 NIV). Pitifully, Gideon responded, "My clan is the weakest in Manasseh, and I am the least in my family" (v. 15 NIV). But God convinced Gideon to move from victim to victor. The result: Gideon led Israel to victory over the intimidating Midianites.

Jeremiah, who some call "the weeping prophet," suffered from deep and abiding insecurity. Surely mocked and scorned for his struggle, he told the Lord he didn't know how to speak—his intimidation by men threatened to keep him from achieving his kingdom purpose. However, God answered, "Before I formed you in the womb I knew you, before you were born I set you apart, I appointed you as a prophet to the nations" (Jeremiah 1:5 NIV).

Commentator Canon Cook said of Jeremiah,

> We find him sensitive to a most painful degree, timid, shy, hopeless, desponding, constantly complaining and dissatisfied with

the course of events, but never flinching from duty. . . . Timid in resolve, he was unflinching in execution; as fearless when he had to face the whole world as he was dispirited, and prone to murmuring when alone with God. Judged by his own estimate of himself, he was feeble, and his mission a failure; really, in the hour of action and when duty called him, he was in very truth "a defenced city, and an iron pillar, and brazen walls against the whole land" (1:18). He was a noble example of the triumph of the moral over the physical nature.[1]

King David's son Amnon lusted for his half-sister Tamar—he was so determined to have her that he was sick with passion. Chillingly, he pretended to be ill, then asked David to have Tamar bring him food. Once she was in his room, he sent the servants out; consumed with lust, he said, "Come lie with me, my sister." Tamar, mortified to realize that her own brother would act so dishonorably, begged him to relent, but Amnon, refusing his opportunity to turn from evil, overpowered and raped his sister, bringing her unimaginable shame:

> Tamar put ashes on her head, and rent her garment of divers colours that was on her, and laid her hand on her head, and went on crying. And Absalom her brother said unto her, Hath Amnon thy brother been with thee? but hold now thy peace, my sister: he is thy brother; regard not this thing. So Tamar remained *desolate* in her brother Absalom's house. (2 Samuel 13:19–20)[2]

This Hebrew word for "desolate" is the term *shaw-mame'*, meaning "to stun, stupefy, devastate" or grow "numb." Tamar's trauma devastated her to the point of emotional paralysis, which is common among the abused. However, remember this: Unlike Tamar, you and I have the power of the indwelling Spirit to heal us from such lifelong anguish.

Healing from trauma does take time, yet many victims are continuously harassed *because* they've not realized their God-given kingdom authority and instead are focused on merely getting past life's next pothole. Unable to see past their problems, they become so enmeshed in the victimization vortex that in time they think *survival, not victory* is the normal Christian life. Arthur Burk writes,

> This attitude is totally understandable. Scripture says, "Hope deferred makes the heart sick." While it is understandable, it is not permissible. Obtaining freedom from victimization requires us to appropriate God's power. God delights to make his power available to us, but only for kingdom objectives. He is not primarily interested in helping us to survive. He wants to partner with us in releasing his power into our world in such a way that we become life givers to others around us. It is about building up and expanding, not survival.[3]

EVERYONE IS EMOTIONAL

As noted earlier, victimization isn't gender-biased—it happens to both males and females. Think of the thousands of boys and girls who've been violated by priests. How many of them will escape the victim mindset? Furthermore, without a powerful, transforming work in them by the Lord Jesus, some will themselves become abusers. One of the devil's primary schemes is to perpetuate victimization.

The problem with childhood sexual abuse isn't remembering you were abused; the problem, rather, is trying to forget it. Know this: *Once God heals the pain, the memories are only just that—memories.* No pain. No ache. No terror.

Our emotions only react; they can't think, organize, or plan. Emotions are *involuntary* responders to our circumstances. They are either positive or negative in nature: excitement vs. despair, pleasure vs. displeasure, faith vs. fear (for example). There's no neutral ground—we may *seem* to be unemotional or passive, but even an absence of emotion (apathy) is an expression of emotion! We all manifest some level of response (seen or unseen, perceived or unperceived) to life's situations.

We need to understand how our emotions work because *emotional responses correspond to our personalities.* Since emotions are reactors, when we think strongly about an issue, we generate strong feelings about it. Our emotions trigger our will to act. Whether we reflect light or reflect darkness depends in part on how healed we are from past wounds.

EMOTIONAL DEVELOPMENT

No one is born with a full set of healthy emotions; we gradually learn to differentiate between them:

- From birth to three months a child experiences various measures of distress or delight.
- From three months to six months a child begins to demonstrate fear or anger.
- From six months to twelve months a child learns to express affection and elementary love.
- From twelve months to eighteen months a child experiences more complex feelings (such as jealousy) or has behavioral issues.

Each of us progressively develops patterns of emotional responses or expressions. Our subconscious mind, the platform of our thinking, is networked and programmed through repetition. If we undergo abuse or endure fearful conditions (trauma) on a regular basis (repetition), our mind registers impressions that form habits based on experience.

Emotional		Expression
Anger = Younger	>	Tantrums, screaming
Anger = Older	>	Sulking, rebelling, raging, cursing, irritability, withdrawal, bad grades, behavioral problems
Fear = Younger	>	Hiding, shyness, crying, thumb sucking, bed-wetting, fear of the dark

Fear = Older	>	Drug abuse, sexual issues, isolation, antisocial behavior, physical problems, performance-orientation
Envy = Younger	>	Bullying, teasing, name-calling, threats, temper
Envy = Older	>	Criminal activity, manipulation, critical spirit, fury, harmful actions

Babies and toddlers are naturally self-centered. They love to see themselves in a mirror, they want the toy for themselves, and their language revolves around "me" and "mine." They simply express their happiness, contentment, anger, or fear.

Teenagers express an increasingly broader array of emotions as they learn how to be unselfish, kind, and respectful. Each expression of love is on its own emotional level—one love for football, another love for parents—and teens are prone to perceive themselves according to how they're treated. An overweight teen bombarded with teasing is likely to establish a mental pattern of *I deserve this*. Next, she punishes herself by gaining more weight, and her wounded spirit begins to send out a "vibe" that she's desperate for acceptance and affirmation. This unseen SOS can then be perceived by any predator who would take advantage of her.

If we're emotionally healthy, by late adolescence and into adulthood we will distinguish between truth and falsehood, goodness and evil, justice and mercy. Mature Christians desire to prove themselves honorable before God and others. Nevertheless, some abuse victims actually look for ways to be exploited, because that's all they know; victimized people often heap shame and disgrace on themselves without realizing it.

Several years ago a Jenny Jones show featured women who thought they had hot bodies (gorgeous figures). As I sat in my living room, taking a break from work, I was drawn by the sheer audacity of some of the guests. One woman thought she was the spitting image of drop-dead-gorgeous Oscar-winner Halle Berry. Now, Halle is a *looker* (in Texas that means she's beautiful), so stunning that she pulls top billing in Hollywood's highest-grossing films. Believe me, the girl on Jenny's show was *no* Halle Berry.

This confused young lady boasted of the resemblance, though she was about one hundred fifty pounds overweight, and that was the least of her problems. As she preened on the runway with prissy hip-action, the audience booed and hissed in obvious disagreement with her personal assessment. It was painful to watch the supposed look-alike argue with everyone in the studio who tried, usually with gentle-ness, to tell her the truth. Finally, one slender, clean-cut young man jumped to his feet, determined to be heard: "Girl, sit yo'self down! Someone done *lied* to you!" Well, friends, the devil is *the* liar—he's often lied to me, and he's probably lied to you too. Let's set the record straight!

The devil never plays fair, but he does play for keeps. Where he gains a *toehold* in our lives through fear, falsehood, trauma, injustice, betrayal, or generational iniquity, he will develop a *foothold,* which will ultimately become a demonic *stronghold,* unless we do something about it.

God has given us unique personalities with a specific purpose to fulfill our kingdom assignment on this earth.[4] The devil wants to kill, steal, and destroy our belief in the truth (John 10:10); to remain a victim puts a person at risk of losing sight of God's purpose.

THE VICTIM SPIRIT

If after being traumatically victimized our thinking becomes pol-luted and we develop false conclusions and convictions, these can man-ifest in illicit behaviors such as overeating, lying, violence, chemical abuse, adultery, phobias, excessive spending, or sloth. I refer to a "victim spirit" on two different levels.

First, I use the term *victim spirit* to refer to the (human) spirit of a person who's been violated in some way and, whether intentionally or unintentionally, has failed to process the experience properly. A person who embraces the victim mindset keeps the victimization pattern recurring, unless, or until, it's broken. I'm not referring to everyone who's been abused; only to those who continue believing lies and thereby allow evil to shape their lives. A victim, for instance, can explain why it's right for things to be wrong, continuing to allow access to an abuser, such as a woman who excuses physical abuse by her husband: In her mind, she thinks she is the problem and that she deserves to be beaten.

Or a boy who continues to accept bullying or harassment without standing his ground and speaking out for his intrinsic worth: In his mind, he's worthless and he doesn't merit anything else.

Second, a *victim spirit* can refer to any one of a host of unseen demonic spirits who are attracted to and desire to attach themselves to a person who will embrace their lies and behaviors, accepting a victim identity. An unseen world of darkness filled with spirit beings is looking for an opportunity to harass and torment you.[5] When victimization produces trauma, demons often attach themselves to the wounded individual to advance the diabolical cycle of events. The victim's fear, intimidation, and hopelessness are now satanically supercharged.

Terms used to describe demonic activity in an individual are:

- *Demon obsession:* mental or emotional obsession caused by an evil spirit, often involving confusion, hallucination, fantasy, hearing voices in the mind, and paranoia.
- *Demon oppression:* experience of feeling pressed down (physically, mentally, and/or emotionally), characteristically yielding to depression, lethargy, chronic fatigue, and sometimes suicidal thinking.
- *Demon possession:* Although the King James Version uses the word *possession,* the original Greek word means "demonized," describing

a person in whom a demon dwells. The Holy Spirit dwells in the believer's spirit; demonic spirits dwell in a person's soul (mind, will, and emotions) and/or body.

A demonic spirit of victimization has a voracious appetite: It must be fed to stay in place, and it thrives on unforgiveness, fear, abuse, and self-condemnation. Though many victims (especially children) played little or no part in being victimized, the enemy is shrewd— he'll whisper to abused people that they're at least partially responsible for the pain they've suffered, and if they believe him, they're trapped, unable to heal, move forward, and grow.

It's natural for us to yield to bitterness and resentment toward those at whose hands we've suffered. *Embracing a wrong mindset always precedes the demonic;* if we fail to forgive, then a gate to our life is opened to demons. This isn't something I made up. Jesus said it. (We'll later talk about this more fully.) To have fellowship with the Lord we must repent of *our* wrongs and receive God's forgiveness— the bitterness and resentment in us is *our* responsibility.

Sometimes we find it easier to accept God's forgiveness for the one who abused us than to accept His forgiveness for ourselves. Why is it so hard for us to forgive ourselves? Because of our pride or our ignorance of human nature, we often reason that we shouldn't have sinned or allowed sin to happen to us. Take note of this: To do so is to argue that sin is extraordinary for us, that we're not prone to sin, or that we are too spiritually mature to sin. Wrong. Sin is natural to us; we never become so spiritually mature that we're unable to sin. Any one of us is a breath away from sin at any time. It's only by God's grace and our perseverance that we don't sin. We should always be mindful of our proclivity to sin, and therefore guard our hearts.

Peter was one of Jesus' closest friends—he, James, and John walked more closely with the Lord than anyone. We know Peter best for his radical, or reactionary, approach to almost any situation—like when he jumped in to defend Jesus and cut off the ear of the high priest's servant. While we tend to focus on how Peter began to sink in unbelief once he was walking on water, he's the only person we know of (other than Jesus) who *has* walked on water!

I'm sure you remember how impetuous Peter pledged his faithfulness to Jesus, then promptly denied Him three times. How do you face the shame of denying your Savior in His most difficult hour after having been one of His dearest friends? Easy for us to say, "Jesus forgave him." Yes, He did! But for Peter to access forgiveness from the Lord, he had to acknowledge that he needed it, that he had actually committed the sin that required it.

Instead of groveling in self-pity, Peter came to believe the truth that John would later write: "If we confess our sins, He is faithful and just to forgive us our sins, and to cleanse us from all unrighteousness" (1 John 1:9). Peter was *convinced* of Christ's forgiveness; it's Peter who later encourages us to keep a clear conscience (1 Peter 3:16) and reminds us that God gives grace to the humble (5:5).

I assure you right now that your loving Father in heaven has a wonderful plan for you, even if through life's difficulties you've lost sight of it. I urge you to make the investment to read the rest of this book—all of it. Allow my witness of God's glorious victories to become yours as well.

For now, consider your emotional well-being. You may have to look back into your childhood or adolescence, or maybe your glance backward is only a few years past. Do you see where you developed unhealthy emotional habits? How? What happened to initiate this? Was it the result of a trauma? Or sin? Or harmful words? Or fear? Or rebellion? Take time to ask the Lord to reveal the root issues of your emotional pain. Write down anything He shows you. Later we will take opportunity for you to repent, renounce open doors, and break any contracts you may have made with darkness.

The next chapter will challenge you, but I pray that you will read and apply its principles. If you do, you will have a fuller understanding of how life-altering experiences can either open a door to abuse and victimization or—praise God—to freedom!

CHAPTER FOUR:
Life-Altering Experiences

In November 1963, seventeen-year-old Laura Welch borrowed the family car to attend a party with friends. A few hours later, the Welches received the call parents dread: Local hospital staff told them Laura had been in an accident. She never saw the stop sign, so she drove through the intersection at normal speed, plowing into a car that had the right-of-way. Laura suffered only bruises, but the driver of the other car—a local high school track star and Laura's good friend—died on impact.

Laura would later say that this tragedy shaped her perspective on life at a young age, bringing new compassion and wisdom. Her friends and family marvel at her serenity and strength, and you also may have grown to respect her qualities as an adult. Laura Welch went on to become Laura Bush, wife of President Bush.[1]

You and I have experiences every moment of the day. Most aren't in and of themselves life-altering—they're the mundane occurrences most everyone consistently encounters. However, one major event *can* be life-altering, just as recurring experiences accumulated over time affect our course. The resultant changes can be for good or bad, and, as with Laura Welch Bush, the person undergoing the experience determines the ultimate outcome.

The devastation left in the wake of Hurricane Katrina was life-altering. People who went through it will never be the same. One old woman, found holding her dog atop a tree down the street from her home, explained to a reporter that she'd never considered herself to be "religious," but now "that has all changed." She had a life-altering encounter.

Those who survived the shock and fear of the December 2004 tsunami in Asia will forever be affected. Some turned to devils and idols for comfort; some sought the living God; others became bitter and angry. What these people underwent in their crises will be life-changing. Will they be better people for the experience? They alone will determine that.

What sets a life-altering experience apart from an everyday experience is the reality that life has been altered, changed—a transformation has occurred. These come in two "colors": holy and unholy.

Holy life-altering experiences turn our hearts toward God. They shape us, even if only slightly, into the image of Christ. They consist of . . .

- personal decisions we make for Christ;
- experiences we have with Christ during prayer or Bible study;
- the influence of and association with godly people;
- shared experiences with other Christians that produce holy soul ties, spiritual bonds for life (unless otherwise broken); (A holy soul tie is an invisible thread, an unseen connection tying together hearts and lives through prayer, service, and ministry to one another.)
- tragedies that compel us to seek and turn to God;
- situations in which we throw ourselves on God's mercy in repentance;
- emotionally traumatic experiences that cause us to call for God's help;
- events that build our faith to stand against adversity;
- sickness or deathbed encounters where God visits us.

Unholy life-altering experiences turn our hearts away from God. They cause us to lose sight of His intentions for us and faithfulness to us. They consist of . . .

- decisions we make to deny Christ access to and control of our lives;
- willful choices to submit to spiritual darkness, either through rebellion or willful sin;

- the influence of and association with ungodly people;
- shared unholy experiences with others that produce unholy soul ties, spiritual connections for life (unless otherwise broken);
- tragedies that provoke us to blame God;
- traumatic events that cause us to feel abandoned by God;
- situations that build our fear and mistrust;
- occurrences that create emotional instability in us.

"COVENANT EXPERIENCES"

Life-altering experiences are profound covenant encounters. "Covenants with whom?" you might ask. That's the point: The choice is ours (with the exception of those too young to understand or regulate the dynamics of their experience).

Through *holy* experiences we can establish spiritual covenants with holy people. Over time, partners in the service of Christ build lifelong relationships with one another. Consider a pastor and his wife who have served in the same church for many years. Years in relationship with the congregation have woven together the fibers of their lives into a beautiful divine tapestry. The pastor and his wife are part of the congregation, and the congregation is part of them. The godly covenant is made on two levels:

- They have entered into a holy soul tie covenant with the people they have served.
- They have entered into covenant with God through their years of faithful service. The Lord's anointing rests upon the couple in greater and deeper levels as they continue to surrender to Him in obedience.

A scriptural instance of holy covenant is seen in the case of Jacob's parents, who, in keeping with custom, sent him out to find a bride for himself. Along the journey, Jacob stopped to sleep, and while he slept he had a dream in which God told him that the land he was standing on would belong to him and all his descendents. When he awoke, Jacob realized that he'd had a life-altering encounter—he would never be the same. He took a stone on which he had been sleeping, poured oil on it, and made a covenant with God. The promise he received from God forever changed his point of view, his sense of purpose, and his priorities in life (see Genesis 28:12–22).

Unholy contracts are made with unholy people. Through force—violation, assault, abandonment, or cursing, etc.—those who choose evil actions traumatize those who are young and/or weak. From this vulnerable place they cower in fear as victims. Ungodly connections can be formed (for example) through fornication, adultery, homosexuality, bestiality, group sex, and rape; these are not only sins against God but also against our own bodies.

Whether we know it or not, when we enter into ungodly and unholy contracts, we enter into covenant on two levels.

- First, we enter into covenant with the person(s) with whom we've engaged in sin, willingly or unwillingly. This soul tie is an unseen connection that ties our hearts and lives together with evil and can leave doors open to our lives that must be shut. Jehoiada, a priest from the house of Judah, is a biblical example of one determined to break unholy contracts:

  Jehoiada then made a covenant that he and the people and the king would be the Lord's people. All the people went to the temple of Baal and tore it down. They smashed the altars and idols and killed Mattan the priest of Baal in front of the altars. . . . [Jehoiada] also stationed doorkeepers at the gates of the Lord's temple so that no one who was in any way unclean might enter. (2 Chronicles 23:16–17, 19 NIV)

- Second, we enter into covenant with spirits of darkness who provoke sin in us and feed on that sin, which often in turn results in some level of demonization. Demons use unholy soul ties to connect their evil activity to a person.

Even unwillingly entering a partnership with evil opens the spiritual gates of your life to further assaults—this happened to me and thousands of others to whom I've ministered. It's common for a victim to allow and even (knowingly or unknowingly) invite spirits of injustice, evil, and wickedness into his or her life due to the open doors of wrong associations. *A covenant is established in the spirit realm until one party breaks it;* you will have to break the covenant to see change occur. (More on this later.)

Western Christians have little understanding of the unseen world. After thirty-five years of dealing with the demonic, I find it tragic that the church is largely focused on the use of medicines and psychology to help free Christians from emotional and mental problems. There are certainly times when medicine and counseling are in order, and thank God we have skilled men and women who can help many in our society, but why is it that we often turn immediately and primarily to the medical field rather than to Jesus Christ for our breakthrough? In my personal and professional experience, much freedom can be achieved with revelation of the truth, through forgiveness, through severing covenants with darkness, and through walking in the light.

ANATOMIES OF LIFE-ALTERING EXPERIENCES

Illustration #1

Billy gives his heart to Christ at eight years of age. One year later, someone at school attempts to sexually seduce him. Billy tells his teacher and parents, and tragedy is circumvented. Because Billy made wise and right choices, God's storehouse of blessing is opened to him:

"The eyes of the LORD are everywhere, keeping watch on the wicked and the good" (Proverbs 15:3 NIV). There was no sexual violation, no unholy contract with an unholy person, and no door was opened for the demonic. Because of Billy's commitment to truth and purity, his life-altering experience with God protects him from evil.

At twelve Billy attends a church camp and surrenders his life to foreign missions. His encounter with and submission to God's call profoundly affects him. His surrender honors the Lord, and he receives additional revelation about God's purposes and plans for his life. His choice invites the covering and ongoing blessings of heaven. Right choices move God.

Peter quotes David when he writes, "The eyes of the Lord are on the righteous, and his ears are attentive to their prayer; but the face of the Lord is against those who do evil" (1 Peter 3:12 NIV, from Psalm 34:15; see also Psalm 26:3).

Years later Billy chooses a godly wife. Again the Lord is honored; emotional, spiritual, and financial blessings follow. Doors open to godly associations. Billy receives favor before men in his service as a missionary. He is achieving his life goals.

None of us is perfect. And even though we all at times will be subject to wrong choices, whether or not we humbly repent of our sin can open or close spiritual doors. Placing the Lord on the throne of our lives hinders the advancement of darkness against us.

Illustration #2

Johnny is a boy who suffers from both physical and emotional abuse. There's no one to guide him, so he becomes embittered and angry. The spiritual door of his life is thrown open to darkness. Believing lies about himself and God, he concludes, "I'm nothing but damaged goods. I'm worthless. I'll never amount to anything." The demonic world labels him a *victim* because he verbally condemns himself and displays the presence of broken emotions.

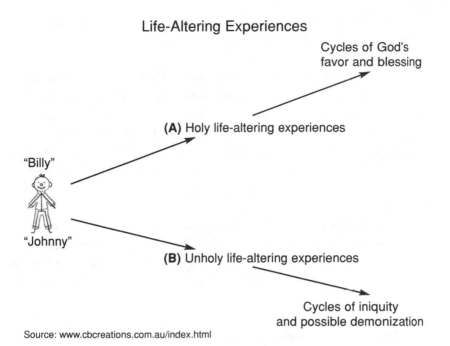

Life-Altering Experiences

Cycles of God's
favor and blessing

(A) Holy life-altering experiences

"Billy"

"Johnny"

(B) Unholy life-altering experiences

Cycles of iniquity
and possible demonization

Source: www.cbcreations.com.au/index.html

Once the door is ajar, unless there's someone who knows how to conduct spiritual warfare and facilitate inner healing for Johnny, he quite likely will experience further unholy life-altering violations. As he becomes older, Johnny will continue in ungodly patterns, establishing cycles of iniquity. (Iniquity is defined as *gross injustice, wickedness, and evil*.) The result of his unforgiveness and bitterness is that Johnny is cut off from God's blessings, and the demonic cycles will continue, worsening with time.

Illustration #3

Eight-year-old Jillian is raped by an adult neighbor and doesn't tell anyone. Her wealthy parents travel constantly and aren't around to help. Like a wounded animal, Jillian becomes timid and fearful, and, as with Johnny, the spiritual door of her life is left open. She is too young to know how to close the spiritual doors, or know the door is there, or guard or stop the cycle that's begun. She is primed for further abuse.

As a teen, Jillian is offered marijuana. To numb the emotional pain from her earlier abuse, she accepts it. Rejection takes root in her heart, and her drug abuse is exacerbated. One night while stoned on drugs, Jillian is date-raped, resulting in pregnancy. Her parents are furious; to protect themselves and the family from further embarrassment, they send her to a home for unwed mothers until she gives birth. Each unholy life-altering experience deepens her entrenched belief that she will always be a victim.

There will never be a change in Jillian's abusive life cycle until she takes control, identifies the lies she's believed, repents for believing them, and comes to the saving knowledge of Christ. She must then choose to be free of her tormentors and take those life-giving steps to freedom.

When a person comes to Christ, he or she is transformed from the kingdom of darkness to the kingdom of light. However, the contracts, covenants, and alliances made through past traumas and sins remain; Christ *is* the answer, but the new believer may not know how to access the freedom. My friend Arthur Burke says (and he's absolutely right), "The good news is, living with a victim spirit is totally optional." I've written this book to help you find your freedom, break your cycles of harassment and sin, and take your stand in Christ.

Although as an innocent child I was sexually, verbally, and emotionally assaulted, I took responsibility for my problems. I spent many hours in prayer, allowing the Lord to heal my human spirit, deliver me from the entrapment of predatory spirits, and to free me from a faulty mindset. There's an investment to be made if you are to enjoy God's fullness. If you want victory in your life, you'll have to take personal responsibility. You didn't deserve the abuse you received, but that doesn't mean you must live a defeated life. Get up and take action.

If you allow Him, the Lord will use what you've experienced, both good and bad, to purify you! When refining gold, the refiner melts and then stirs the gold over heat until all its impurities float to the top. He skims off the impurities and turns up the heat, and then repeats the process, all the while increasing the heat. Molten gold is pure when the refiner can see his reflection in it.

Prayer, surrender, death to self, fasting, praise, and an intimate relationship with Jesus will bring the impurities of abuse, pain, rejection, and trauma to the surface, where the Holy Spirit can remove them. Just as Moses came down from the mountain shining with the Lord's glory, so we will come from the place of prayer reflecting the glory of Christ, having been with Jesus.

When we've been through the fire of pain, our first response should be to nestle under the shadow of the Almighty and draw close to Him. Regardless of the circumstance, if we will respond to God with pure devotion, we will be changed, and others will see His presence and glory reflected in our lives.

PERSONAL HOLY LIFE-CHANGERS

My first holy life-altering experience was when I walked a church aisle at age seven to "get saved." I walked with my friend Judy that morning, who *was* saved. I was certainly sincere, but I wasn't born again at that time; sincerity doesn't save you, Christ does. He has a time and a place for your birth into His kingdom, and that wasn't mine. Nevertheless, because I thought I must be a Christian now (having obeyed the counsel I was given), I didn't behave in negative ways I might have otherwise—I knew the fear of God, but I didn't know God personally.

At age thirteen I had an encounter with the Lord, but I didn't understand that it was the Spirit convicting me of my need to be reborn.

Then in February 1965, at fifteen, I was truly transformed. Surrendering my heart to Christ that night was like walking out of a dark closet and into the sunlight. I sold out to Jesus the day I met Him. I was literally on fire for Christ.

Fasting and praying for my future husband was another step of submission and obedience, a life-altering experience that kept God's blessings and favor on my life.

One of my most significant life-altering experiences came in 1970, around two-thirty one morning. I began my prayer time by reading a page from my favorite devotional book, followed by a passage from the Bible. Next I laid on the floor to pray, and for twenty or thirty minutes I praised the Lord Jesus for every detail of my life. Suddenly this memorable wee-hour experience was interrupted by a heavenly urge to *let go*. Let go of what, I wasn't sure. But the Spirit came in such power that I couldn't move.

As I wept before Him, the Lord asked me, "Alice, where is the altar you have built for me?" This confused me, and I didn't know what He was asking. Then the Spirit reminded me of experiences men and women had in the Bible: life-transforming encounters as a result of sacrificing to God on an altar, usually an altar they had built for Him.

Altars in early times were often built in certain spots hallowed by a religious or spiritual association with God. They were places of sacrifice and surrender. So I built an altar in my heart that night and presented myself as the sacrifice—a *living* sacrifice.

That altar changed my life forever. As some did in the Old Testament, I gave it a name: "The Lord Is Present." There I learned that the best arguments and opinions of man could never invalidate my experiences with the Lord. Or, as my late father-in-law taught me, "A person with an experience is never at the mercy of a person with an argument."

Early that morning in 1970, as I sacrificed myself, my dreams, my husband and children, my possessions, and my ministry to the Lord, I was converted from living for myself to living for God's kingdom. As I relinquished everything in my life to His control, I was filled with His Holy Spirit. I will never be the same again.

An altar is a place of sacrifice and death, so *beware of building an altar in an attempt to get something from God.* Sacrifices are what we give, not what we get. God will never allow us to manipulate Him toward our own ends. Life isn't a *Let's Make a Deal* show—rather than choosing which curtain or door we'll walk through, we experience it as it comes. It's what we do with the experience that eventually makes us who we are!

"Sacrificing" something to the Lord to receive something in return is no sacrifice at all. Exodus 20:25–26 (NIV) says,

> Do not build it [an altar] with dressed stones [human plans], for you will defile it if you use a tool on it. And do not go up to my altar on steps [pride and self-promotion], lest your nakedness be exposed on it.

Any true sacrifice is void of self-interest. Sadly, most of us know sacrifice only in theory, not in reality.

Have you built a holy life-changing altar to God? On it, were your eyes opened to see Him in a way you'd never seen Him before? If not, build an altar to Him today; climb upon it and ask for heaven's fire to consume you and for revelation to change you. *You* will never be the same!

TAKING SPIRITUAL INVENTORY

It's time to take spiritual inventory of your life. You've likely had holy and unholy life-altering experiences, encounters that have molded your present and can influence your future. Unholy experiences that haven't been reconciled leave the spiritual door of your life ajar and allow the enemy to harass, stalk, and torment you. Holy experiences— godly acts of worship, service, surrender, and humility before the Lord Jesus—build you up and keep the door of heaven's blessings and God's favor open to you.

Now is the time to evaluate yourself. Make an honest assessment of where you are. It's never too late to cancel covenants you've made with darkness. It's never too late to begin building altars to the Lord and experiencing Him in new, fresh, and transforming ways.

List your experiences. Take your time and don't rush—allow the Lord to remind you of them. Ask Him to reveal what you don't or can't remember. Let this day be a life-altering experience for you!

Holy Altars	**Unholy Altars**
My Life-Altering Encounters With God	My Life-Altering Encounters With Evil
1.	1.
2.	2.
3.	3.
4.	4.
5.	5.
(and more)	(and more)

Regarding your unholy experiences, pray:

Father, in the name of Jesus Christ, I repent for allowing unholy life-altering experiences to keep me bound to covenants of abuse and victimization: (Name each one). *I'm sorry that the gates of my life were entry points for further sin and ongoing violations, and I repent to you now. I'm sorry for allowing the abuse to continue without doing anything about it. Forgive me for not seeking your help earlier for the breakthrough. Forgive me for blaming you and others for my problems. I receive your cleansing from my past. I receive the anointing, by your mighty Spirit, to step out of this vicious cycle, and I praise you for the victory and joy and open doors to come.*

Open your eyes and say this aloud with authority:

Powers of darkness, in the powerful name of Jesus, the name that is above all names, I command you to loose me now. I break all contracts, alliances, cults, sects, bloodshed, unholy altars, curses, rebellion, agreements, and unholy soul ties with the demonic. Now! . . . Go! I belong to Jesus and not you. You no longer have any legal right to me. I send an eviction notice to you. Leave my home, leave my possessions, leave my family, and leave me.

I am no longer your victim—and I never will be again. Be gone!

Regarding your holy experiences, pray:

Heavenly Father, I bless you for the experiences that drew me to your love—they have been life-altering. I bless you for showing me the way to be saved. I am so grateful. Thank you for the time when (thank Him for specific spiritual experiences that you know altered your life to serve Him). *You are a good and faithful heavenly Father. I love you so much, and I dedicate my life to you now, afresh and anew. I need you every minute of every day, and I praise you for lifting me from the place of darkness and into the light. In the mighty name of Jesus Christ I pray. Amen.*

CHAPTER FIVE:
Strongholds: Holy and Unholy

Arthur Gordon tells the story of a man, stricken with polio at age three, whose Depression-poor parents had abandoned him at a New York City hospital. Taken in by a foster family, at six he was sent to stay with their relatives in Georgia, in hopes that the warmer climate would improve his condition.

What actually improved his condition was Maum Jean, an elderly black woman who took that "frail, lost, lonely little boy" into her heart. For six years she daily massaged his weak legs, administered her own hydrotherapy in a nearby creek, and encouraged him spiritually with her stories, songs, and prayers.

> Night after night Maum Jean continued the massaging and praying. Then one morning, when I was about twelve, she told me she had a surprise for me.
>
> She led me out into the yard, placed me with my back against an oak tree; I can feel the rough bark of it to this day. She took away my crutches and braces. She moved back a dozen paces and told me that the Lord had spoken to her in a dream. He had said that the time had come for me to walk. "So now," said Maum Jean, "I want you to walk over to me."
>
> My instant reaction was fear. I knew I couldn't walk unaided; I had tried. I shrank back against the solid support of the tree. Maum Jean continued to urge me.
>
> I burst into tears. I begged. I pleaded. Her voice raised suddenly, no longer gentle and coaxing but full of power and command. "You can walk, boy! The Lord has spoken! Now walk over here."
>
> She knelt down and held out her arms. And somehow, impelled by something stronger than fear, I took a faltering step, and another, and another, until I reached Maum Jean and fell into her arms, both of us weeping.

It was two more years before I could walk normally, but I never used the crutches again. . . .

————————

[Many years later] the night came when one of Maum Jean's tall grandsons knocked on my door. It was late; there was frost in the air. Maum Jean was dying, he said; she wanted to see me.

The old cabin was unchanged: floors of cypress, windows with wooden shutters—no glass, roof of palm thatch mixed with pitch. Maum Jean in bed, surrounded by silent watchers, her frail body covered by a patchwork quilt. From a corner of the room, a kerosene lamp cast a dim saffron light. Her face was in shadow, but I heard her whisper my name. Someone put a chair close to the bed. I sat down and touched her hand.

For a long time I sat there. . . . Now and then Maum Jean spoke softly. Her mind was clear. She hoped I remembered the things that she had taught me.

Outside, the night stirred with a strong wind. In the other room the fire snapped, throwing orange sparks. There was a long silence; she lay with her eyes closed. Then the old voice spoke, suddenly stronger, "Oh," said Maum Jean, with surprising gladness. "Oh, it's so beautiful!" She gave a little contented sigh, and died. . . .

————————

All that happened a long time ago. I now live in another town. But I still think of Maum Jean often, and the main thing she taught me: Nothing is a barrier when love is strong enough. Not age. Not race. Not disease. Not anything.[1]

Like this man, you too can walk. You can walk out of emotional pain from past abuse. Jesus has shattered the barriers; our problem is our difficulty believing that we can be victorious. For breakthrough, it's critical that you break free from your old mindset and embrace (take in, put on) the mind of Christ. Press into believing God—your faith moves Him—and examine these spiritual principles, truths that can help you conquer the victim mentality and move into a life based on faith.

STRONGHOLDS

Simply put, strongholds are systems of thinking. The idea is this: What you believe forms your thoughts. What you think determines your actions, your speech, and eventually your health. Again, there are holy strongholds, which God builds with truth and from which He operates, and there are unholy strongholds, which the devil builds with lies and from which he operates.

A military stronghold, an entrenchment from which an army can wage war, begins as an invading or defending force and gains a beach-head or foothold. Most historians agree that the war against the Axis Powers (Germany and Italy, on the European front) was won on D-Day, June 6, 1944, on the beaches of Normandy in France. When the Allied Forces of the U.S., Britain, and Canada landed, the casualties over a six-day period were brutal: 37,000 dead, 172,000 wounded or missing. Terrified courage joined to steel-jawed determination gave our men the advantage; if they could win that beachhead they could take the front lines inland and ultimately defeat the fascists. That victory is largely responsible for the freedom Europe enjoys today.

In spiritual terms, a holy stronghold is a belief system that accepts as true the will of God as it is expressed in the Word of God. It begins as a truth, becomes lodged in your heart, establishing a "beachhead." From there the Holy Spirit adds revelation and builds a holy stronghold in your heart.

David wrote:

The LORD is my light and my salvation—
whom shall I fear?
The LORD is the *stronghold* of my life—
of whom shall I be afraid? (Psalm 27:1 NIV)

59

The Hebrew word for "stronghold" is *maw-oze,* which means "a fortified place, a rock and defense." When you allow the truth of the Word to settle into your spirit, God makes that truth become experiential for you.

Since Christ is your fortress, rock, and defense, you can find refuge in Him. At salvation, you received His mind (cf. Philippians 2:5); now it's your job to surrender your thinking to His and find renewed confidence in God's stronghold.

Let's look at passages that show us how we can build a holy stronghold.

> Once you were darkness, but now you are light in the Lord;
> walk as children of light—lead the lives of those native-born to the
> Light. (Ephesians 5:8 AMP)

A person born and raised in a town knows the back roads, the neighbors, the subculture, the favorite restaurants, and so on—it's his natural habitat. The apostle Paul is saying that we who believe upon Jesus Christ have been moved from the kingdom of darkness into the kingdom of light. So walk, live, and operate in your life as though you've only known the light!

Begin to live this out. Give a gift of encouragement to a struggling friend. Invite people to your home for food and fellowship. Share your faith. Pray for those around you. You aren't that old person anymore, so do these things (or carry out similar actions) instead of spending your time and money as you once did. You're a new creation, native born to the Light!

> [Give] thanks always for all things unto God and the Father in
> the name of our Lord Jesus Christ. (Ephesians 5:20)

How do you live this verse? Say an unexpected bill comes in the mail—do you praise the Lord anyway? The Spirit is able to work on your behalf when you act on God's directive to praise Him in all things. What happens? Maybe the phone rings and a woman on the other end apologizes for sending you an already paid bill—you don't owe them anything. Every opportunity for living the truth establishes a beachhead from which your situation can change. Instead of living as a victim again, you are developing a mindset of truth.

> His divine power hath given unto us all things that pertain unto life and godliness, through the knowledge of him that hath called us to glory and virtue. (2 Peter 1:3)

Each day, aloud, thank the Lord that you are receiving all things that will add to a fuller life in Christ.

Picture this: One day you're sitting in freeway traffic when your car overheats and stalls. You're frustrated, but you believe that God can bring something good from the situation. You begin to praise God right then. A man who sees your plight comes over to help. After pushing the car onto the roadside, you ask to use his cell phone to make a call. When you mention that you're calling your brother, Johnny Davis, for assistance, he asks if you mean the Johnny Davis who's a member of Praise Community Church. You answer yes, that's your older brother. He excitedly says that Johnny and he are prayer and study partners, that he thinks the world of Johnny.

After you hang up, your new friend asks about your vocation; your detailed answer leads him to tell you what God is doing with his business, *and* that there is no doubt in his mind God set all this up to meet you. Right there on the freeway shoulder, he offers you a job with his company. . . .

Or, sometimes nothing happens at all. Maybe the Lord is simply testing your faithfulness in the midst of difficulties. Trust Him to know what's best for you at all times, and act on the truth to honor and obey Him.

Live out the truth by acting in faith. Scriptural revelations are beachheads from which the Lord is able to graft His truth into you and set you free. It's more than a play on words to say a stronghold is a hold on your life that's strong; Jesus Christ is the strong one to whom you can hold and who will hold on to you!

Here are some biblical beachheads:

- I am a king and a priest unto God (1 Peter 2:9; Revelation 1:6).
- I am free forever from condemnation (Romans 8:1).
- I am free from sin's power to rule over my life (Romans 6:1–6).
- I have been made righteous (2 Corinthians 5:21).
- I am complete in Christ (Colossians 2:9–10).
- I have been raised up and seated with Jesus in heavenly places (Ephesians 2:6).
- I have direct access to God through the Spirit (Ephesians 2:18).
- Jesus Christ is in me (Colossians 1:27).
- I have been saved and set apart for God's glory (2 Timothy 1:9).
- I have the right to go boldly before God's throne in prayer (Hebrews 4:16).
- I am a partaker of God's divine nature (2 Peter 1:4).
- I have been established, anointed, and sealed by God (2 Corinthians 1:21).
- I was chosen by God, before the world's foundation, to be holy (Ephesians 1:4).
- I am redeemed, forgiven, and have received full grace from God (Ephesians 2:5).
- I will have all my needs met in Christ (Philippians 4:19).
- I am no longer in the dark, and I now walk in the light (Ephesians 5:8).
- I have every spiritual blessing available to me (Ephesians 1:3).
- I have been given the mind of Christ (1 Corinthians 2:16).
- I have been spiritually perfected in Christ (Hebrews 10:10).
- I belong to God, and I am not my own (1 Corinthians 6:19–20).
- I've been predestined, called, justified, and glorified in Christ (Romans 8:30).

In summary: When we accept such truths into our belief system, a beachhead is established in our minds. From this the Holy Spirit builds His stronghold in us as we allow God's truth to influence our thoughts, beliefs, and behavior. In the process, the Spirit cultivates truth in our hearts and exposes the devil's deception, revealing the false identity we have embraced. The holy stronghold becomes the foundation on which our victorious life is built.

I once heard a story that in many ways illustrates a holy beachhead.

> A circus acrobat, asked about the safety net below him, jokingly admitted that the net underneath the trapeze artists was there to keep them from hitting the ground and breaking their necks, but he added, "I'm glad we have the net because it also keeps us from falling.
>
> "You see," he explained, "If we didn't have the net, we'd be so nervous when performing our feats that our minds would be constantly focused on falling, not on performing. We have the courage to attempt two turns or maybe even three—all thanks to the net!"

It's true: Trusting God is the safety net by which we can love others, forgive those who have wounded us, allow the Spirit to go to the root of our pain, and fully live. Our security in the Lord Jesus is the net of His love. Reach out, accept the truth, believe it, and live it.

To establish holy strongholds in my life, I wrote into a spiral notebook Bible quotes (like the ones above) that I could *read aloud* every day. I memorized these and many other verses for when circumstances called for "the mind of Christ." Some of the verses I stuck on my bathroom mirror, others in my car, and some on my refrigerator. Try it! Dare to break free from the lies that say you'll never change. You can do it, and God's unfailing arms will catch you if you should slip.

In the mid–1980s, a woman in my cell group struggled terribly with abuse from her past. After a meeting one night she initiated a one-on-one conversation with me. I asked her what was going on.

Tears rolled down her cheeks as she said, "God doesn't love me." Marcy (not her real name) had come from a broken home; her parents had divorced when she was quite young. She remembered the physical and verbal abuse she and her mother and little brother had suffered as though her life had frozen in the time of her childhood.

The pain in her voice reflected her ongoing mental rehearsal of the rejection and lies she'd believed all these years.

"Marcy, you know how I've been teaching you about believing the truth of God's Word? And about who you are in Christ?"

"Yes," she said, sounding not at all convinced.

"I want you to read your notes to me, aloud. What do they say about who you are?"

As Marcy began to read, her despair gradually changed to a glimpse of hope. She could hear herself say, "I am complete in Christ," and something triggered in her heart. I could see it in her eyes.

"Do you believe those verses are true about you, regardless of your past, regardless of your feelings, without changing one thing about yourself?"

She hesitated a few seconds as she thought through the teaching. Then, as if a light bulb had just illuminated the words, she said loudly, "That's amazing! The Word of God is true, and it's true for me. I am complete in Christ, but I had believed the lie. No longer— I get it! I really see it! Before the foundation of the world, these truths were established. I just needed to believe and receive the truth. Wow!"

None of Marcy's circumstances had changed. However, her understanding of who she was in Christ *had* changed, which would change her beliefs as well.

UNHOLY STRONGHOLDS

Once more: An unholy stronghold is a state of mind that accepts as true something contrary to the will of God as expressed in the Word of God. As holy strongholds are built on the truth of the Word, unholy strongholds are built on Satan's lies: "'[The devil] was a murderer from the beginning, not holding to the truth, for there is no truth in him. When he lies, he speaks his native language, for he is a liar and the father of lies'" (John 8:44 NIV). When we accept a lie about God, others, or ourselves, we have the potential for allowing an unholy stronghold to form. These are built from mental repetition (meditation) of lies, fear of every kind, personal sin, wrong belief systems, generational strongholds, or abusive situations. That's why we *must* let the meditation of our hearts be acceptable unto God (see Psalms 19:14; 49:3; 119:97).

The devil knows how to use beachheads in our lives. When we believe a lie about God's ability to redeem our past, an unholy beachhead is formed, and a stronghold, like a house of thoughts, begins to be built. The enemy might begin by implanting thoughts such as *You're so ugly. No one loves you. You deserve what they said about you.* As you accept the lies, meditating on them and rehearsing them over and over, your mental torment increases.

Soon the accuser convinces you that the lie is really the truth, and the lie becomes reinforced through your words and actions. It's only a matter of time until your shaky foundation gives way and you are victimized again. Once you believe what is false, what you hear, see, or do is filtered through the lens of that false belief. One battle invites another, and in time you sabotage your relationships because you've rejected yourself and others. Satan's beachhead of lies has become a stronghold (see 2 Corinthians 10:3–5).

HAGAR AND ISHMAEL

Perhaps you're familiar with the story of Abraham, Sarah, and Hagar, the Egyptian maidservant who bore Abraham the son he named Ishmael. But did you know it was Hagar's wounded spirit that opened the door of victimization for an entire culture, an effect that continues to this very day?

Abraham's wife, Sarah, deeply desired to have a child, and when she felt there wasn't any hope for conception, she had Abraham sleep with Hagar. The tension between the two women was obvious once Hagar became pregnant (Genesis 16:4). For Hagar despised Sarah, and Sarah, disgusted with Hagar's haughtiness, quickly sent her away.

An angel found the rejected and bitter Hagar near a spring in the desert beside the road to Shur. Interestingly, Shur means "a wall"— often what's happening in the natural correlates with what's developing in the spiritual. I believe Hagar, the mother of Ishmael, the father of Israel's eventual enemies (e.g., see Genesis 16:7–11), developed a wall of offense toward Sarah and Abraham that set into motion the animosity that has never failed to set Arabs and Israelis at odds.

"I'm running away from my mistress Sarah," Hagar told the angel, who told her to go back and submit: "You are now with child and you will have a son. You shall name him Ishmael ['God hears'], for the Lord has heard of your misery" (v. 11 NIV). When Ishmael was born, he and his mother lived with Abraham and Sarah.

The day came when Sarah gave birth to Isaac, the son of promise (see Galatians 4:28). In Genesis 21:8 we learn that a party was given for Isaac on the occasion of his weaning, and the wounded victim spirit that began its work in Hagar's heart appears to have been transferred to Ishmael: "Sarah saw that the *son* whom Hagar the Egyptian had borne to Abraham was *mocking,* and she said to Abraham, 'Get rid of that slave woman and her son, for that slave woman's son will never share in the inheritance with my son Isaac'" (vv. 9–10, NIV).

Disappointed, Abraham sent Ishmael and Hagar away. The two wandered in the desert of Beersheba ("Well of the Oath"), and she sat the child under a tree while she went to another place to weep. The Hebrew word for "weep" suggests she was wailing and lamenting in loud, distressful cries of bitterness. The Lord heard Hagar and even more so the cries of Ishmael. He assured Hagar that Ishmael would become a great nation.

With every open door of offense, there is always a God-promise you can receive from Him if you choose. In Hagar's case, God opened her eyes to see water that she could give Ishmael to save his life in the desert. If you will ask Him to open your eyes, your offenses can be washed clean by the living water of His promises too.

Unfortunately, Hagar didn't deal with her unforgiving and wounded spirit. Ishmael picked up her bitterness and perpetuated it as well. Scripture reveals that Ishmael's mocking attitude set a course of history that is still operating today. (Genesis 25:18b NIV says, "and they lived in hostility toward all their brothers.") Unless you step over your wounded spirit and walk in victory with Christ, like Ishmael, you will affect future generations of your family with the same wrong spirit you've embraced.

One day two monks were walking through the countryside on their way to another village to help bring in the crops. As they walked they spied an old woman sitting at the edge of a river. She was upset because there was no bridge and she couldn't get across on her own.

The first monk kindly offered, "We will carry you across if you would like."

"Thank you," she said, gratefully accepting their help. So the two men joined hands, lifted her between them, and carried her across the river. When they got to the other side, she thanked them again and went on her way.

After they had walked another mile or so, the second monk began to complain. "Look at my clothes," he said. "They are filthy from carrying that woman across the river. And my back still hurts from lifting her. I can feel it getting stiff." The first monk just smiled and nodded his head.

A few more miles along, the second monk griped again. "My back is hurting me so badly, and all because we had to carry that silly woman across the river! I cannot go any farther because of the pain."

The first monk looked down at his partner, now lying on the ground, moaning. "Have you wondered why I am not complaining?" he asked. "Your back hurts because you are still carrying the woman. But I set her down five miles ago."[2]

This is what many of us are like in dealing with our past—we're that second monk who can't let go. We hold the pain over our loved ones' heads like a club or we stay trapped in our critical spirit, and all the while unholy strongholds bind us like the graveclothes of Lazarus.

Regardless of how victimized we've been in the past, perpetuating lies will open our gates to further problems. This happened to Hagar and Ishmael, and many Arabs today around the world still live in constant hostility with others. In the next chapter we'll examine how the sins, attitudes, or actions of our forefathers can still affect us today.

CHAPTER SIX:
Iniquitous Patterns

I was a Realtor in the eighties and early nineties. I love the different styles of homes, and selling them I was able to meet and influence many people. The long hours and the occasional testy client might cause one to question my passion for the task, but for years I was a top-selling agent in the Houston market. In 1994, the Lord called me into a full-time speaking and writing ministry. It was a difficult decision—I loved selling homes—but once I entered the ministry, I could no longer continue my real-estate business.

One transaction of particular interest to me illustrates the existence and impact of iniquitous generational patterns. I had serviced a one-year lease for a homeowner, and at the end of the year the renters were still occupying the property. Two months later, fourteen months after the original lease, the renters called the owners, saying they'd purchased a home and wanted to move without penalty. The owners had assumed that because they hadn't heard from the tenants they were planning to reside in the property one more year; the owners asked me if they had any legal recourse.

I explained that in our state, when a renter stays in a property one day beyond the termination date of the lease without prior written arrangements, the lease is automatically renewed for another year. Because the renter didn't satisfy the contract by notifying the owners in writing, the existing, binding lease was extended. On their own, the owners filed a civil suit against the renters, and I was asked to be present in court along with the owners' attorney. The judge quickly awarded the homeowners the case, ruling that the renters were legally bound to the contract *and* to rent money for the additional year.

Consider this concept as applied to the spiritual realm. Again, the devil never plays fair, and he holds millions of Christians responsible for yesterday's leases. We may be believers who love the Lord while still being obligated to the devil for past contracts that were never satisfied and, more important, never cancelled. Unfortunately we've assumed that Christ's sacrifice for our sin automatically nullifies pacts we've made with the powers of darkness. Not so. *Jesus' sacrifice reconciled us to God; we are still responsible to cancel contracts we've had with darkness.* Until we do, the enemy has the legal right to enforce the agreement.

You may have had addictions, committed sexual sins, fallen into stealing or lying. Perhaps your parents have rejected God. Or maybe you've struggled with depression and suicidal tendencies, like others in your family have. Maybe you've experienced physical, sexual, verbal, or emotional abuse. You're a Christian, and you know Jesus Christ is alive in your heart, yet you can't seem to break free from the past. *Why?*

GENERATIONAL ISSUES

We need to know what we are speaking of when we talk about an iniquitous generational stronghold, or generational iniquity. Let's consider definitions.

Generation comes from the root *genesis,* which means the origin or beginning of something. The study of *genetics* relates to the origin and development of one's ancestors or progenitors that establish and stimulate traits in one's development.

Bottom line: Who and what your parents and grandparents (and so on) were in their lives directly affects who you become. This applies beyond hair and eye color—it also impacts your personality, mannerisms, expressions, even your character strengths and weaknesses. Yes, even your tendencies toward specific sins.

For example, my parents went through the Great Depression in the 1930s, when food, water, clothing, and other provisions were scarce. My daddy, the baby of nine children, lost his father when he was only five. His mother worried that the children would not be cared for, so she made sure they didn't waste anything. Daddy in turn never wasted anything, and my parents carefully saved money for the future.

You can probably identify with this too. You may have an elderly relative who won't throw away even a morsel of leftover food, or is obsessed with keeping old (even expired) coupons and empty aluminum cans (intended for recycling, though rarely carried out). How their family members dealt with the conditions of the Depression era continues to impact their behavior today.

Now for the spiritual dynamic: The word *iniquity* is used 262 times in the Bible. A generational stronghold is an influence, open door, or trait that causes us to think, believe, and behave in a manner contrary to God's truth. It may be a mental programming system or a demon connected to a family (familial spirit) that provokes and perpetuates repeated behaviors from generation to generation.

> The LORD is slow to anger, abounding in love and forgiving sin and rebellion. Yet he does not leave the guilty unpunished; he punishes the children for the sin of the fathers to the third and fourth generation. (Numbers 14:18 NIV)

> Thou shalt not bow down thyself unto them [idols], nor serve them: for I the LORD thy God am a jealous God, visiting the *iniquity* of the fathers upon the children unto the third and fourth generation of them that hate me. (Deuteronomy 5:9, emphasis added)

> [God keeps] mercy for thousands, forgiving *iniquity* and transgression and sin, and . . . will by no means clear the guilty; visiting the *iniquity* of the fathers upon the children, and upon the children's children, unto the third and to the fourth generation. (Exodus 34:7, emphasis added)

> You show love to thousands but bring the punishment for the fathers' sins into the laps of their children after them. (Jeremiah 32:18 NIV)

The Lord is slow to anger, patient with us (2 Peter 3:9), and He desires for us to live in freedom from iniquitous patterns of the past. One Hebrew word for *iniquity* (*aw-vone'*) means "perversity," moral "evil," "mischief," "punishment" (of iniquity), "or sin." Another word, *aw-vaw*, means "to be crooked, bent down with perverseness." Iniquity is a propensity toward sin, a tendency to follow the same path. Although we are only guilty for our individual sins (see Ezekiel 18:18–20), the proclivity to repeat the behaviors of past generations is very present, and the responsibility to identify and break these patterns is ours.

If I were to plant a young sapling tree in my front yard, in time its root system would develop. If while playing in the yard my grandson happened to step or fall on the base of the young tree, it would become bent, and the tree would continue leaning to one side until Eddie straightened it and secured it with rope and stakes. "As the twig is bent, so grows the tree"—this is the way generational iniquity works.

One family member opens the door to alcoholism . . . habits develop . . . patterns form . . . one or two generations later, other members are caught in the same trap. As that generation yields to the same familial spirit or entertains the same mental programming, they "renew the lease" their forefathers made with evil. Scripture teaches that leases of generational iniquity extend three to four generations! You might say, "But the third and fourth generation since Adam is long ago." Yes, but if you have one family member who renews the lease of generational sin in the third generation, then the iniquity is perpetuated into another three or four generations. *Someone,* finally, must take it upon himself to break the lease and cancel the contract.

Jesus was aware of generational iniquity, as were the people of His time.

> As Jesus passed by, he saw a man which was blind from his birth. And his disciples asked him, saying, Master, who did sin, this man, or his parents, that he was born blind? Jesus answered, "Neither hath this man sinned, nor his parents: but that the works of God should be made manifest in him" (John 9:1–3).

His reply shows that in this case the man's blindness was not the result of a generational iniquity, which implies that it was possible for this to have been the case.

The work of the cross is finished, but if we don't live according to the positional truth of who we are in Christ—the status of having received His righteousness through His sacrifice—then the devil will always take advantage, continuing to impose the old system on us. My favorite apostle, Paul, tells us in Galatians 3:13 that Jesus redeemed us from "the curse of the law"; however, the consequences of sin still operate if we don't do something about them. He also admonishes us to "stand fast therefore in the liberty wherewith Christ hath made us free, and be not entangled again with the yoke of bondage" (5:1). If there *were* no yoke of bondage to be concerned about, Paul wouldn't need to instruct us as such.

Consider what he says in Romans:

> Reckon ye also yourselves to be dead indeed unto sin, but alive unto God through Jesus Christ our Lord. *Let not sin therefore reign in your mortal body, that ye should obey it in the lusts thereof.* Neither yield ye your members as instruments of unrighteousness unto sin: but yield yourselves unto God, as those that are alive from the dead, and your members as instruments of righteousness unto God. For sin shall not have dominion over you: for ye are not under the law, but under grace. What then? shall we sin, because we are not under the law, but under grace? God forbid. *Know ye not, that to whom ye yield yourselves servants to obey, his servants ye are to whom ye obey; whether of sin unto death, or of obedience unto righteousness?* (6:11–16, emphasis added)

Sin doesn't have dominion over us any longer! *But,* if we yield to unrighteousness we become its slave. We renew the lease! Even as a new creation in Christ, remaining a slave to the old life is possible, if we allow it. It's our choice.

To better understand iniquitous generational patterns, imagine a spiritual umbilical cord. It is like the unseen contract that has attached people to their family lineage. When I had my children, the first thing the doctor did was cut the umbilical cord—my babies couldn't have lived on their own if he'd left it attached.

It's similar in the spiritual realm. When we're reborn, the cord of the family—its tendency toward sin, abuse, unforgiveness, and victimization—must be severed. Again, receiving Christ and His salvation reconciles us to God and removes the guilt of sins we've committed, but if we don't also cut that "family cord," the devil will continue to work through the old life we lived and the iniquitous patterns we've inherited.

My first revelation of how generational iniquity can be established came to me in the early eighties. Eddie and I have four precious children; however, during our marriage I lost three babies before they were born. The first was a boy, and I lost him at five months of pregnancy. Then, before our youngest daughter was born, I had two more miscarriages.

One day while praying and asking the Lord to speak to me, the Holy Spirit revealed that I had believed a lie about the loss of my children—a generational lie from my mother's side of the family. (I want to be very clear that not all miscarriages are about generational iniquity. Sometimes, for instance, a woman has a weak uterus, prohibiting her baby from being supported properly; an RH blood factor can also affect a fetus. If you have any connection to miscarriage, only the Lord can reveal to you if your situation is like mine.)

I was *shocked* by what I discovered when I looked at our history: a serious ongoing problem stemming back as far as my great-grandmother. She lost two children, one still birth and another by miscarriage. My grandmother's first child was stillborn. Then she had a miscarriage before she gave birth to my mother. When she was forty-five, she gave birth to my aunt, then she died only six years later. One grief she bore was the loss of her babies. And, like me, my oldest sister miscarried three children. My mother didn't miscarry, but sometimes a generation is skipped for reasons that can't be explained.

The Lord showed me that *our family had made a pact in the spirit realm, believing the lie that we would always lose babies.* As a family, we'd unknowingly embraced a falsehood that had victimized us for years, regarding something to be true that was really a lie. That day of unveiling an unholy stronghold was a grand day for me because I finally said, "Enough is enough." Will you say the same?

BREAKING FREE OF THE OLD MAN

Neil Anderson, in *Overcoming Negative Self-Image,* offers an example of how we can be programmed wrongly.

> When I was in the navy, we called the captain of our ship the Old Man. My first Old Man was a bad person, and nobody liked him. He drank with the chiefs, belittled his junior officers, and made life miserable for the rest of us. He was a lousy Old Man. But if I was going to survive on board that ship, I had to do so under his authority, relating to him as my Old Man. Then one day he got transferred to another ship. I no longer had any relationship with him, and I was no longer under his authority.
>
> We got a new skipper who was very different. How do you think I related to the new Old Man? At first I responded to him just like I had been conditioned to respond to the old Old Man. As I got to know the new skipper, I realized that he was a good man. But I had been programmed for two years to react a certain way when I saw a captain's braids. I did not need to react that way any longer, but it took several months to recondition myself.[1]

Your family has an Old Man too, and its "spiritual DNA" is programmed to keep you defeated, bound, and victimized. The old man you're dealing with may be a system of thought you've adopted from a parent or a relative. It could be a demonic attachment, an evil familial spirit that's moved through family generations. Regardless, through Christ's blood, through the power of God's Word, and through the authority you have in Christ, you can break free from the "Old Man" system and establish a promise of God's blessings for generations to come.

Before he began to rebuild the devastated city of Jerusalem, Nehemiah repented for his sins, the sins of his countrymen, and the generational iniquities of his fathers (see Nehemiah 1:5–11). King David confessed the sins of his forefathers as well (see Psalm 106:6–8). They certainly were not guilty of wrongs that others had done, but they repented as ambassadors, representative members confessing and asking God to cleanse their families' names from those offenses.

This isn't about shifting blame to your parents or other ancestors—it's about your breaking free from generational bondage. Beware of becoming superstitious with the idea that there's some magical cure to everything. Instead, allow faith to rise up in your heart, and as the Lord gives you direction, repent of your sins and the sins of your family.

Indicators of generational iniquity are behaviors, beliefs, or illnesses that are generationally repeated. What manifestations might reveal such issues in your family? Consider: family covenants (secrets), female mutilation, oaths, vows given by rituals, fear, perfectionism, premature deaths, abortion, accident-proneness, miscarriages, abandonment, all forms of abuse, lying, members having lived as vagabonds or constant wanderers (can't stay in one place or with one job or with one spouse), depression, insanity, poverty, sexual perversion, addictions (gambling, stealing, drugs, overeating, alcoholism, greed, power, lying, sex, bulimia, hoarding), sicknesses, suicide, rage, lawlessness, dysfunction, religious legalism, etc.

To break the power of generational iniquity in your life and in your family, pray:

> *Father, in Jesus' name, I repent for my family and for myself. As Nehemiah repented for his forefathers, and as King David repented for his, I repent for mine. We've sinned against you, grieved you, and looked to other remedies instead of to your healing power. And, Father God, I ask you to cleanse and heal every facet of our family line, all the way back to Adam, that as a family we might glorify and honor you in everything. In Jesus' name. Amen.*

Open your eyes and say this aloud, with authority:

Familiar spirits, in the name of Jesus Christ, whose name is above every name and who has all authority over you, I break any generational curse and iniquity of (name the issue), between me and my *father*, and his mother and father, all the way back to Adam.

I break any generational curse and iniquity of (name the issue), between me and my *mother*, and her mother and father, all the way back to Adam. I lay an axe to the root of the unfruitful tree of sin and darkness, and I command you to loose me and leave me, NOW! I belong to Jesus Christ and not you! I cut you off, root you out, and evict you, NOW . . . be gone!

Identify and renounce each issue separately. Continue until you sense God's peace and a breakthrough.

Pray this with me:

Father God, I welcome your sweet presence. Fill and empower me to express a clear and victorious testimony of what you do in a life surrendered. Thank you for the change I'm about to experience in my life and in the life of my family. In the powerful and wonderful name of Jesus. Amen.

CHAPTER SEVEN

The Vicious Cycle of Lies

In her insightful book *Overcoming Bitterness,* Gwen Mouliert writes about perceptions of past memories as a child.

A bitter spirit has an acute memory, but that memory may be riddled with irrational distortions. I can quickly recall things from my childhood that hurt me. Not only can I recall them, but the details seem to be indelibly etched on my mind. (Is the same true for you? Be honest.) However, a few years ago, I would still have argued with you that my early home life was a healthy one. I remembered the hurtful things that directly affected me, yet I denied that as a family we had any problems.

I first became aware of this destructive pattern several years ago when my older brother and I had dinner together. He lived in Florida then, and I took him out to dinner to celebrate his birthday and just to spend some time with him. During the meal, we shared some of our favorite stories from our childhood.

To my utter amazement, we had two totally different interpretations of the same events—in fact, the memories of much of our early home life didn't line up at all. My brother opened up to me about how disturbing and disquieting our childhood had been. Even now as an adult, some of those things still affected him. For my part, this sounded so foreign. Where had I been when all of this was taking place? My brother is five years older than I am, but from our different perspectives, you would have thought we grew up in different cities and were raised by different parents.[1]

Memories Become Meditation

When abuse of any kind occurs, memories form. Over time our minds often either diminish or exaggerate because our ability to remember is imperfect. This is one reason why accident and crime investigators interview witnesses on the scene or as soon as possible.

As we meditate on our memories (whether accurate or inaccurate), our emotions engage, and we can easily build a house of lies about the situation or about ourselves. For instance:

- We may assume new identities—as "victims." We may mistakenly assume that our experiences define us, determining who we are. (Not true.)
- We may judge and demean ourselves. Because we've mentally embraced the idea that we're "worthless damaged goods" (not true), we may behave and speak derogatorily about ourselves. This affects the way we dress, the friends we make, and the things we do. We lose self-respect.

Stand-up comedians sometimes demean themselves to disguise the possible pain of their past. Recently there was a reality TV show called *Last Comic Standing*. One of the funny guys was Ralphie May, from Houston, who has a southern drawl that makes me sound like I'm from the Midwest. He's around five-foot-three and weighed over three hundred pounds. Ralphie used his weight as the butt of his jokes; even though he made the audience laugh, I felt that deep inside he was in emotional pain. Recent reports say he has had gastric bypass surgery to correct his weight, which he'd always managed with humor.

- We may fall victim to false guilt. Absorbed in denial, agony, or escape, we sometimes assume we deserve the abuse we've received, otherwise it wouldn't have happened. (Not true.)
- We might blame God for what happened. It's easy for us to forget that we live in a fallen world where men and women may choose to be ungodly. We assume God controls people. (Not true.) Humans aren't puppets—we have moral freedom for which we, not God, are responsible.
- We may believe the Lord abandoned us in our trauma, therefore He can't be trusted. (Not true.) I'm surprised by the number of

people at the altar asking for prayer, yet admitting they can't trust God with their lives; past experience has caused them to be cautious and defensive. God *didn't* abandon you—He grieved with you.

• We conclude that everyone is out to get us. (Not true.)

Meditation Becomes Mindset

As we meditate on memories, whether accurate or inaccurate, our meditation establishes a mindset. As attitudes are formed, mental strongholds are built. Unseen signals are sent, like when young boys secretly tape signs to each other's backs that say, "Kick me!" It's as though there's an invisible invitation on us that sends out subconscious signals to others, saying, "Abuse me, please." Evil people and evil spirits read the messages sent by our body language or words.

Mindset Produces Abusive Behavior

The Bible says, "As he thinketh in his heart [meditation], so is he" (Proverbs 23:7). Once you've meditated long enough on your trauma, the cycle of abuse, like poured concrete, becomes set; you will attract and yield to more abuse from others because you now feel hopeless, helpless, and defeated. Negative words fall from your mouth—just as faith comes by hearing (see Romans 10:17), despair comes through condemning words, and the more you say the words, the more you believe them. As the powers of darkness pick up on your cowering posture, your fatalistic words, and your facial expression, they influence you to become antisocial.

Unable to see your downward spiral, you might begin to dress and act in ways that put others off while you withdraw from or avoid meaningful relationships. Gloomy and defeated, you may resort to self-destructive actions that become seemingly uncontrollable, building in momentum (through demonic empowerment). Often the abused becomes an abuser:

(1) Eating disorders (anorexia, bulimia, bingeing, excessive fasting, etc.)
(2) Self-mutilation (cutting, tattoos, piercing)
(3) Damaging behaviors (overeating, stealing, drugs, suicide, rage, criminal activity, nicotine, alcohol, sexual sin, perversion, etc.)

DEALING WITH PAIN

When you've been subjected to trauma, whether from verbal criticism and put-downs, physical beatings, abandonment, sexual abuse, or satanic abuse, your emotional responses reveal the ways you're coping with the pain. Here are three typical human reactions.

REDIRECTION

One approach we take is to redirect our attention, change course, or go the opposite way to avoid or postpone the anguish. A man in pain may become a workaholic—shifting his focus from his woundedness to his work—to avoid difficult emotions. An angry woman may become depressed and give up on life by taking drugs or drowning herself in food. Others resort to abusive behavior, taking out their fury on their spouse or children. One may become the "all-American guy" who wins the trust of others, takes their money, and then skips the country with millions. Many sink into despair, shutting down internally, withdrawing from life, and becoming vulnerable to spiritual oppression.

> I am the spirit of depression! I dwell only in people who have their gate open for me to walk into their lives. I dwell in all kinds of people . . . successful people, failures, and wealthy people.
> People who are going through some hard knocks . . . people who have lost their jobs, have broken marriages, their car won't run,

the rent is due, and they're out of money. But, I also manage to walk through left-open gates of people who are read up and even prayed up.

When allowed to stay by the persons I indwell, I am able to spread doom and gloom in their life, extract the joy from their walk, bring great pessimism, and create a cynical attitude. . . . I am able to produce sluggishness, tiredness, sleeplessness, loss of appetite and of course devastation to the spiritual life of the person. I am, in fact, one of Satan's most effective strategies to neutralize true believers and render them ineffective for long periods at a time.

I am the spirit of depression! There is no life I won't enter, given the invitation of the open gate. The only people I can't touch are those believers whose commitment to Jesus Christ is the highest thing in their life . . . people who spend daily time in prayer and the Word . . . people who never miss church and who are involved in ministering to others. Those folks are off limits to me . . . there is nothing I can do to get to them, but I won't stop trying. Meanwhile, I continue to indwell those with the open gate. I AM THE SPIRIT OF DEPRESSION! I will enter anyone, anytime, any way when the gate of his or her life is unguarded. I am the spirit of depression.[2]

After evaluating a man who sought him out and made an appointment, the psychiatrist concluded, "Sir, you're suffering from a classic case of depression. My prescription, though, is rather unorthodox: I want you to attend the circus that's in town. The ads say their clown is world-renowned, guaranteed to make *anyone* laugh."

The man dropped his head in disappointment and sighed. "You don't understand, Doc. I *am* that clown."

So many of us have become skilled at redirecting and disguising. If this includes you, are you willing to close the gates of depression, pain, and abuse? You have been given authority through Christ to take action . . . so go forward. I agree with Neil Anderson's observation: "We are living in an age of anxiety. People all over the world are paralyzed by fear of anything and everything but God. Anxiety disorders are the number one mental health problem in the world."[3] He continues with Chuck Colson's advice: "For the church in the West to come alive, it needs to resolve its identity crisis, to stand on truth, to renew its vision . . . and more than anything else, it needs to recover the fear of the Lord."[4]

Repression

We also often deal with pain by internalizing it. We allow our hearts to be filled with anger or bitterness, and then when we experience a circumstance too stressful for us to bear we may even explode, sometimes with dangerous consequences.

We saw this in the shootings at Colorado's Columbine High School. The actions of Eric Harris and Dylan Klebold resulted in carnage, including thirteen dead and twenty-four wounded. The tragic senselessness of such choices should reveal to us the need for inner healing—we can't afford to let our emotions go unaddressed. Jesus Christ is the healer of broken hearts. True heart change only comes by spiritual transformation (not through the world's methods of handling victims). Instead of seeking help, these two teens, motivated by bitterness and energized by evil spirits, chose to allow their emotions to determine their actions. The results were deadly.

In the aftermath of the shootings, there was a great deal of debate about what motivated the killers and whether anything could have been done to prevent the crime. The reality of social cliques in high schools was a frequent topic of discussion. Many argued that the pair's isolation from the rest of their classmates prompted feelings of helplessness, insecurity and depression, as well as a strong desire for attention. Some schools also began programs to expose and stop school bullying, which many charged had fueled anger and resentment within Harris and Klebold.

They were portrayed as outcast "nerds" who were unpopular and ostracized by much of the school's population; later such characterizations were revised as both Harris and Klebold were documented to have both a close circle of friends and a wider informal social group. However, they were not "popular" and could best be described as being members of the school's "rejects," although by no means were they isolated.[5]

In "The Pain Principle," a chapter in John Maxwell's book titled *Winning With People,* he talks about what he faced as a young pastor with another man who repressed his pain.

Early in my career, I accepted an invitation to lead a church. It was a wonderful opportunity, and it was in a nice town. It was an exciting time for Margaret and me. I had been at the church only ten days when I received a piece of mail from Tom, a member of the congregation. I opened it up, began reading, and soon discovered that it was a typed transcript of the sermon I had delivered on my first Sunday. I was amazed—and flattered—that someone had taken the time to capture every word I had said. And then I looked more carefully. The pages were covered with comments. Tom had red-penned every grammatical mistake, corrected every misspoken word, and pointed out anything he thought was a factual error.

I thought it was odd, but I didn't worry too much about it. I know I'm not perfect, and I'm aware that I sometimes make mistakes when I speak. But I have a healthy self-image, so I didn't let it bother me. But then the next week, another envelope arrived in the mail from Tom. Once again, the message I had preached the previous Sunday had been transcribed. And once again, every tiny mistake was marked in red ink. That's when I figured I'd better meet Tom and find out what was bothering him.

The next Sunday after delivering the sermon message, I asked someone to point out Tom to me. I walked over to him, stuck out my hand, and said, "Hi, I'm John Maxwell."

At first Tom just stared at me. Finally he said, "Hello, *Pastor.*" And that's when I realized he wasn't going to shake my hand. Then he turned on his heel and walked away.

Sure enough, a couple of days later, guess what I received in the mail? Another envelope from Tom. I started calling them his "love letters." I got one every week with his in-depth critique. Would you care to guess how long I received Tom's love letters? Seven years! During that time he never voluntarily shook my hand. I tried to connect with him, but he wanted little to do with me. In only one subject could I get him to engage in conversation with me. Our kids were adopted, and so were his, so he'd talk to me about them. But he wouldn't warm up.

Then one day I had lunch with a veteran pastor. I told him about Tom, the weekly love letters I received, and my inability to win Tom over. My pastor friend looked at me and said, "You know, John, hurting people hurt people." That statement really connected for me. "Whenever someone says or does something hurtful," he continued, "you need to go beneath the surface."

I looked at Tom in a new way after that. I began searching for the cause of his pain, and I tried again to connect with him. Finally one day when I was trying to get him to engage, he made a statement that more than hinted at the problem. He said, "Never trust a pastor." I later came to find out that Tom had once served as a board member at a church and had been mistreated by the pastor. He decided from then on that pastors were bad news and couldn't be trusted.

After I understood the problem, I was able to work on winning Tom's trust. It took a lot of effort, but by the time I left Lancaster to accept another leadership position, Tom had gotten over his mistrust of me. We became friends. And not only was he willing to shake my hand, but he'd give me a great big bear hug. By then, he had long since given up sending me love letters.[6]

Without John's maturity to forgive this man and reach out with love, bitterness could have taken root. How does unforgiveness become bitterness? A root of bitterness occurs when we make judgments about an offense, a situation, words spoken or actions taken against us or against someone we love without properly forgiving and resolving the issue. When our pent-up emotions continue to fester and boil over the same series of circumstances, there is potential for bitterness to take root.

I want you to see that this can be more than a physical or emotional problem: The gates of bitterness open us to a realm of demonic activity that stands ready and more than willing to "super-size" our offense. My friend Cindy Jacobs says it this way:

> The judgments that we make in bitterness actually start a cycle that will cause us to fall into the same set of situations over and over until we deal with the root issues in our lives. Our merciful heavenly Father does this because sin, when it is full-grown, brings death.[7]

So how do we uproot bitterness?

- Make a list of friends, family, boyfriends, girlfriends, business associates, neighbors, or anyone else in your life, including yourself, against whom you might have formed judgments. (Remember: *God* is judge, and when we form judgments, we are attempting to unseat Him.)
- Find a personal accountability partner to whom you can confess your bitterness. Remember, this isn't a gripe session, but a confession session. If you don't have anyone to share with, don't despair. God is a friend that "sticks closer than a brother" (Proverbs 18:24 NIV).
- Ask the Lord to open your spiritual eyes to any bitter-root judgments that continually cycle in your life (e.g., "All men are controlling like my father," or "White people like Mr. James are always racists"). Make the list of what the Lord shows you.
- Pray and release (don't ask the Lord to release—*you* release) the person who has hurt, offended, or violated you. A victim spirit is one where the same thing happens over and over. (Also, we'll discuss forgiveness issues in more detail later.)
- Name them one by one and forgive them. Ask the Lord to forgive you for judging them. To refuse to forgive a person is to say to Jesus Christ, "Lord, it was nice that you shed your blood on the cross as payment for the sins of the entire world. However, your dying wasn't enough to pay for the sin _____ did

to me. Come down from your throne, Jesus, and let me sit there so I can judge those who've hurt me." Is that what you really want to say?

- Now, out loud and with authority, say to the powers of darkness, "I break the bitter-root curses that I've embraced as a result of judging others."
- Next, ask the Lord Jesus to cleanse you with His cleansing blood. Pray something like:

> *Precious Lord Jesus, I apply the powerful blood of your sacrifice right now. Please break all the bitter-root judgments in me, and apply the sweet fragrance of healing to my spirit, mind, and emotions. Lord, show me how to love and serve _____. Wash me now. In your name. Amen.*

Self-"Medication"

Some try to appease their deep-seated hurt with unnecessary legal drugs or illegal drugs, Internet addictions, violence, romance novels, adultery, masturbation, cursing, media obsessions, fantasies, alcohol, homosexual activity, or any other distraction to temporarily salve the wounds. These don't cure the hurt—they simply cover it. Inside there are still open, festering sores yet to be healed.

What are some indications that we are unconsciously looking to the wrong things for our healing?

- Weakened morals—lust, adultery, abortion, fornication, cohabitation, pornography—e.g., movies, books, magazines, to arouse emotional responses[8]
- Dissipated energies (these crush mental strength and can also cause physical problems)—rage, pouting, bitterness, domestic violence, distrust, suicidal thoughts, possessive hoarding, hatred, fear, resentment, isolation, cynicism, irritability, animosity[9]
- Physical indicators—chronic fatigue, excessive allergies, ulcers,

colon and intestinal dysfunctions, shortness of breath, high blood pressure, arthritis, headaches[10]

- Habits—alcohol, critical spirit, lying, drugs, gambling, promiscuity, stealing, overspending, perversion, phobias, etc.[11]
- Spiritual gauges—cults, groupies, sects, false doctrine, arrogance, spiritual hypocrisy, religious spirit, legalism, pride, lies[12]

It's your turn. Ask the Lord to give you fresh revelation about yourself. Do you overwork, demand perfection from others, or blame them relentlessly? Do other improper behaviors numb your pain? Do you have a tendency toward bitterness and anger—are loved ones never sure when you will explode next? Are you dependent on drugs, nicotine, or alcohol? Lay all this "junk" at the foot of Christ's cross and let His blood cleanse you. Confess your sin to Him right now (1 John 1:8–9). Let go of everything! Tell the Lord your hurts. Cry out to Him for complete healing. Don't hold anything back. Today is your day of new beginnings. Let your healing begin.

As one who resisted abusive cycles for years, I'd like to paint a mental picture of how liberating it is to be free from torment.

Several years ago I was teaching in Tashkent, Uzbekistan, a former Soviet nation nestled in the heart of the ancient Silk Road. The original Uzbeks were of Persian descent, from what is present-day Iran. The Uzbeks of today are gracious, simple, and humble.

My host invited me to enjoy a day of sightseeing. With the gorgeous high-peaked Ten Shan Mountains on the horizon, the crisp fall air was nothing like the sticky, often humid climate of my Texas Gulf Coast. The snows hadn't yet fallen, so we climbed into ski lifts—I loved the feeling of my legs dangling as we ascended. Up and up the lift moved until we got to the summit. The sheer majesty of God's mountains, casting a colorful hue from the sun, was breathtaking, more than words can describe.

At that exhilarating moment, it was time to stop thinking about the intense ministry schedule I'd maintained for the last eight days. I was spent from teaching and ministering at the altar from 9:00 A.M. to 9:00 P.M. daily. Resting and relaxing in God is an essential precondition for renewing our love to Him. On top of that huge mountain I let go of my tiredness, my concerns, and my problems, and then the large perspective of a vast world opened up to me.

If I'd been focused on the ski lift holding me, or on my fear of falling, or on my terror that I'd be abandoned at the top, my experience would have been wasted. Friend, as long as you are consumed with your past struggles, your mundane daily routine, or your pity party, you will miss the adventures that await you. Join me: Let's go up, up, and away!

CHAPTER EIGHT:
Graphing the Process

One night not long ago Eddie and I were watching Kirk Cameron on TBN. His guest was our friend Joni Eareckson Tada, who became a quadriplegic during a diving accident in 1967; the subject was how to face life's adversities. I marveled at Joni's words of health and wholeness despite being confined to a wheelchair with no use of her limbs. The grace on her amazed us when she said, "This wheelchair is the prison that set my spirit free."[1]

What a powerful statement! I've learned it doesn't matter what the enemy does to try to imprison you. If you make the choice to forgive and focus on the possibilities, not the problems, the cycle of torment can be broken.

Jesus told His disciples this story:

> Once upon a time, there was a king who decided to collect all of his debts. He brought in his debtors and demanded that they pay their bills. One man, who owed the king fifty million silver coins, explained that he was unable to pay his debt. The king immediately ordered that the man, his wife and children, and all that he owned should be sold to repay the debt. The man dropped to his knees and begged, "Have mercy, my Lord. Somehow, someday, I promise I will pay every cent I owe!" The king, touched by the man's plea, relented, graciously cancelled the entire debt, and freed the man and his family.
>
> When the newly forgiven man left the king's palace, he happened upon a man who owed him a small debt of one hundred silver coins. Mercilessly he grabbed his debtor by the throat, choked him, and demanded, "Pay me everything you owe me, NOW!" As he had done, his debtor also dropped to his knees, begging, "Have mercy, sir. Give me some time and I promise to repay you." But the man showed him no mercy. Instead, he insisted that his debtor be

thrown into jail until he paid all he owed.

Some bystanders, who witnessed his harsh treatment of *his* debtor, reported it to the king. The king had him arrested and brought before his throne. "Sir," the king said, "you are an evil man! When you begged me for mercy, I cancelled your debt entirely and set you free. Shouldn't you have shown the same mercy to others that I showed to you?" The king was so angry that he ordered the man to be *released to the tormentors* until he had repaid every cent he owed. "That," Jesus said, "is exactly how my heavenly Father will treat you, if you refuse to forgive those who offend you" (Matthew 18:21–35, paraphrase mine).

See that? *God* will release us to the tormentors if we won't forgive. If you choose to walk in unforgiveness, the most anointed minister in the world can't deliver you from demonic torment. I've found that many in the Christian community want personal freedom but can't get it because they refuse to forgive.

If we're honest with ourselves, we'll admit that an important ingredient of our unreconciled relationships has been not forgiving our abusers and offenders. Broken marriages, tension between parents and children, hurtful words, betrayal among friends, verbal/sexual/emotional pain, physical abuse—wherever these occur, they can leave a residue of bitterness, resentment, and estrangement that can easily take root in our subconscious minds and become a demonic playground.

Many of us try to handle our pain in the following ways:

(1) Avoid the person who's wronged us
(2) Pretend it didn't happen
(3) Exaggerate it—see it bigger than it is
(4) Diminish it—see it smaller than it is
(5) Become bitter and unforgiving
(6) Become an abuser

These *aren't* the answers: God's prescription is based on the one who sacrificed His life to reconcile us. Jesus Christ paid the price for sin—hatred, bigotry, and every form of abuse. Jesus showed us how to forgive and gave us the liberty to do the same.

In the financial world, forgiveness refers to a particular money transaction, as when one cancels a debt. If you obtain a student loan from the U.S. government there is a "forgiveness clause" that allows part of the debt to be cancelled for each year that you work in the field of your training. Amazingly, if you were to die before the loan was fully paid, the remaining portion would also be cancelled.[2]

Regarding victimization, forgiveness is like canceling a debt. When you forgive, you make the willful choice to relate to the offender as though the offense never occurred.

IMPRESSIONS

A memory becomes rooted in our minds by the emotional intensity with which it was recorded. When victimization is radical, even violent, the memory is so deeply recorded that we call it "trauma"; our soul (mind, will, and emotions) registers the trauma and develops defense mechanisms to prevent that pain from reoccurring. Approaching painful trauma from the biblical perspective, Paul tells us,

The weapons of our warfare are not carnal, but mighty through God to the pulling down of strongholds;) casting down imaginations, and every high thing that exalteth itself against the knowledge of God, and bringing into captivity every thought to the obedience of Christ. (2 Corinthians 10:4–5)

Unaddressed memories can become strongholds through intensely emotional incidents. As memories repeatedly resurface (often with blurred and distorted actual details), they become more deeply entrenched through time.

I was young, innocent, and clueless when I was first victimized. Looking back now it's clear I was more fearful, hurt, and confused than angry—at six I didn't dare allow myself to be angry with adults. As I grew older I began to realize what had actually happened, and because similar situations were reoccurring, my fear and confusion gradually gave way to disappointment and distrust. Even when amazing ministry doors would open, I'd cower from God's call on my life. This was my method of escape. I was in mental bondage, fearing that men would always take advantage of me in one way or another.

This is one of the most difficult things childhood abuse produces: Even though I was completely innocent and had done nothing to provoke the offenses, I felt guilty, dirty, tarnished, damaged. I never spoke these thoughts, but in my heart I felt them. I embraced false guilt as if it were real guilt, which produced another dilemma. Cleansing is reserved for real guilt—Jesus didn't die for false sin. Since I bore no real guilt, having committed no sin, no matter how often or sincerely I confessed, I didn't "feel" forgiven.

That's how the enemy plays with a victim's head. Let's look at three ways the Lord can heal our minds.

The Holy Spirit Guides Us Into All Truth

" 'The Helper, the Holy Spirit, whom the Father will send in My name, He will teach you all things, and *bring to your remembrance* all things that I said to you' " (John 14:26 NKJV emphasis added). If you allow it, the Spirit will reveal the truth about your situation and heal your pain.

Corkie, a young married woman with one child, grew up in a solid Christian home and married a man who loved the Lord. But she had a serious problem that brought her to me for counsel. She explained that her father, who she said was a Satanist, had molested her, and she was so convinced of it that she'd filed a lawsuit against him. Although he was found not guilty, the incident broke his heart and came close to destroying the entire family.

"Isn't your father an elder in the Presbyterian church you grew up in?" I asked.

She said yes, but that memories of his satanic abuse first appeared five years earlier during a secular psychiatric counseling session. Red flags immediately came up in my heart. "Corkie, are you saying you didn't remember any of this happening to you before five years ago?"

"That's right. The counselor helped me through hypnosis and rebirthing to see what had happened to me when I was a little girl," she explained.

I told her that I also had experienced an assault as a child, but that the problem with sexual abuse is not remembering it but forgetting it. "Did your dad violate your two sisters?" I asked.

"No. They think I'm completely wrong and that Dad has always been a great father to us."

My ministry team of ladies and I agreed to help her. We met and began to pray. "Holy Spirit, you are the Spirit that discloses. Please go into the depths of Corkie's heart and reveal the truth to her. We ask for your healing power to come and touch your daughter. Lord, we know you reveal to heal, not to hurt. So reveal the truth to her now."

As we continued to pray and wait on the Lord for revelation, suddenly Corkie looked up with tears streaming down her face. "This never happened to me. I'm sure of it! It never happened. What have I done? God is telling me that I believed a lie. I am so sad for the horror I've put my family through."

A few minutes later, joy bubbled up in her soul as the truth encounter cleansed her heart. She renounced the lies, broke the contracts she'd made both with the counselor and with the demonic lying spirit, and then asked the Holy Spirit to come and close all doors to strongholds.

The final result? She called and repented to her father, who forgave her. Corkie apologized to her mother and sisters as well. The family recovered, and after twelve years she is still walking today in the light of the truth. The Holy Spirit will do His job if we invite Him.

God Speaks Peace to Our Hearts

"Peace I leave with you, My peace I give to you; not as the world gives do I give to you. Let not your heart be troubled, neither let it be afraid" (John 14:27 NKJV). The promise of peace from Father God is the answer. The Spirit can deal with the root cause, what we call the "pillar event"—the original event by which the abuse or trauma occurred—when we ask the Lord to reveal where the pain started. "He who searches the hearts knows what the mind of the Spirit is" (Romans 8:27 NKJV). Why? Because "the Spirit searches all things, even the deep things of God" (1 Corinthians 2:10 NIV).

I've heard many stories of family members who watched the digression of loved ones with broken, unhealed hearts. Deception destines them to live lives of recurring victimization unless or until they permit God's Spirit to reveal the pillar event. Left unresolved, victims will identify with their woundedness and pain, living with their felt need to get even. They may submit to thoughts of despair and even suicide—the most selfish act imaginable—a permanent solution for a temporary problem.

Those who choose to be perennial victims will remain earthbound in their relationships with God and others. They'll be forced to run with the turkeys when they could have soared with the eagles. Is this you? If so, don't despair; instead, know that "all things work together for good to them that love God, to them who are the called according to his purpose" (Romans 8:28). Not just good things—*all* things. Once you've been reconciled to God and released your abuser, the abuse you suffered will be redeemed and with all your other life experiences worked together for good.

What you thought disqualified you will become your credentials, just as my experiences qualify me to minister to you through these words. What the enemy meant for evil, God will use for good. Satan's assault on me backfired; the assault on you has backfired too. Glory to God! As you submit to Christ's lordship, what Satan has done to you will cost him more than it's cost you.

Sincere brokenness is necessary if Christ's life is to flow from you. That Satan and sin have broken you through trauma isn't the point. Will you allow Christ's life to flow from your broken life to extend His kingdom and meet the needs of others? Will you allow your brokenness to bring glory to God by helping others? Or will you remain paralyzed by shame, guilt, pain, and distrust?

Perpetrators of abuse frequently threaten to harm their victim if he or she tells anyone what's happened. This lays the foundation for a stronghold of fear.

- Fear that my abuser will hurt or kill me
- Fear that my abuser will hurt or kill my friends or family
- Fear of being abused again
- Fear of people finding out and what they will think of me

Accordingly, victims are often doubly abused, trapped with two problems: the abuse itself, and how to keep the abuse a secret.

The violation of our person causes us emotional instability, which triggers the desire to retreat or escape. The victims' secrets make friendship difficult. Unable to be transparent, victims find comfort in isolation, and the connections they do manage are generally surface relationships. The wounded can't let people into their private world, where their pain rules. Tragically, their open heart-wounds cause them to remain self-focused. They increasingly

- focus on their pain rather than on God's purpose;
- focus negatively on their abuser rather than their calling to heal others;
- yield to negative thinking rather than putting on the mind of Christ.

This results in disorientation, doubt, introspection, and confusion—lives spent wasting time with side issues rather than becoming who they were born to be. Don't forget this: Each of us is born with a kingdom purpose for living and a kingdom potential to achieve.

Whether or not we know this, believe me, the devil does. He hopes that the abuse you've suffered will distract you from God's plan for your life and keep you from reaching your kingdom potential. Do not allow it.

Jesus Is Ready and Able to Heal You Completely

The Spirit of the Lord is upon me, because he hath anointed me to preach the gospel to the poor; he hath sent me to heal the brokenhearted, to preach deliverance to the captives, and recovering of sight to the blind, to set at liberty them that are bruised. (Luke 4:18)

This Greek word for *heal* is *iaômai,* meaning "to cure." The power of a cure is even deeper than healing, for to cure implies a guarantee that something will not reoccur. Jesus gives this glorious promise: The Spirit will cure tormenting traumas and cycles of victimization if you will permit Him.

Combing through the meanings of the original words from this text, an amplification of it can yield a paraphrase like this:

The Spirit of the Lord God is upon me, because he hath consecrated me to preach good tidings unto the depressed in mind or circumstances; he hath sent me to wrap up firmly the pain and bring a cure; to break apart hurt from your heart, proclaiming rapid freedom and deliverance to you from the dungeon where you were yoked or hitched to bondage.

Only the Spirit can reach into your subconscious mind, where the painful memories have been planted from your past, and then illumine them with the truth that delivers you from the dungeon where you've been chained. I experienced this freedom, and so can you.

REOCCURRENCE

When our children were small we had them repeat behaviors like brushing their teeth over and over until they became habits. Repeating an activity forms a habit, whether it's cursing or simply tying your shoes. A friend explained to me that even three years after she'd quit smoking, sometimes she'd catch herself reaching for an imaginary ashtray. There was still a program hidden in her subconscious mind.

We can become so accustomed to acting a certain way that we forget why we do it. Ultimately, we do what we do because we think what we think, and our thoughts are linked to our initial memories of experiences. This is a major concept to apply when dealing with character dysfunction.

When Eddie and I pray for a tormented counselee, we ask the Holy Spirit to retrieve memories so He can sever associative links with pain, grief, and fear. A memory may be intense and sharp, where the event was severe and quick. However, sometimes there are general memories of which the specific details aren't clear. Unfortunately, some counselors feel driven to uncover every memory—they might say that any gap in memory is evidence of a problem.

The Greek word for that concept is *baloney*. Not only are gaps *not* evidence of a problem, but the actual memories themselves may or may not be valid. Then what do we do? We ask the Spirit to reveal the key memories and the necessary truth concerning them. He *will* guide us into all truth—there's no need to conjure anything. He is more than able to bring to remembrance what is needed for total healing.

One day almost two decades ago, I was speaking with one of the pastors with whom we had started a church. Pastor Jeff was young enough to be my son, so there was no need for me to feel intimidated.

Then he stunned me. Looking at me through his bright blue eyes, he said gently, "Alice, why is it that every time I talk to you about the need to change something, you throw up an invisible defensive wall?"

"I don't do that," I said, reflectively.

"Yes, you do. It's really there. And this isn't the first time I have seen you do it. What's the problem?"

I told him I wasn't sure, but I was going to pray about it and find out. That afternoon I went to prayer. "Lord, what about it? Do I have walls around me when it comes to men?" I felt His sweet Spirit acknowledge that it was true.

"Well, Lord Jesus, I don't want to be like this. Where did this come from, and how do I deal with it?" I prayed earnestly.

I heard Him speak to my heart: *This goes back to the six-year-old sexual-abuse encounter.*

Immediately I broke down in sorrow and tears. I was confused. Let me tell you why.

As a small child I had already released and forgiven my abusers to God, although I didn't know Him as my Lord and Savior at the time. When I gave my heart to Jesus at fifteen, I made sure I'd forgiven all my offenders. I'd always felt some distrust of men, but that didn't prevent me from working with them, listening to them, or honoring their insight. Never in my wildest dreams did I perceive this as an open account in my life. I had drawn close to Jesus, the Lover of my soul, who would never violate, abuse, or harm me. My heavenly Bridegroom was my All in all. I knew the spiritual intimacy of the prayer closet. I'd even written a bestseller about intimate intercessory prayer called *Beyond the Veil.*[3]

In addition, I didn't have any bitterness or anger toward anyone— so I was shocked when the Spirit confirmed in my heart that something wasn't right. I called one of our pastors and an intercessor friend for prayer at the church.

Trusting the Lord for the courage to tell them this story, I nervously waited for them to arrive. As we entered the auditorium, I anticipated the enduring breakthrough that was about to happen. I told John and Cindy of the clear childhood memories of abuse that progressed into adulthood and then explained that I was sure the Spirit wanted to do something deeper in my life. (What, I wasn't sure.)

They'd not prayed long when Pastor John made a simple statement that to this day still packs a punch: "Alice, I now release you from the shame and false guilt of the abuse you suffered as a six-year-old girl."

I fell facedown on the floor and cried and cried. I don't remember anything else they said from that moment on. All I know is that those words reached into the depths of my spirit and soul. They freed me from my fear of abuse and the ache of how it opened doors to other types of continuing abuse.

After two hours of weeping I felt drained, exhausted, overwhelmed, and delivered. The Lord had performed spiritual surgery that went far beyond my mind, will, or emotions; it extended into the core of my being . . . my very identity.

We said our good-byes, and I sat there for a few minutes. My eyes were swollen almost shut.

In the car on my way home, I distinctly recall asking the Lord, "What just happened to me? I thought I'd dealt with this issue many years ago." What He showed me that day has now helped thousands of people.

The reason I had to revisit this trauma was that when I was a brand-new Christian, I had only a shallow view of God's love and of my covenant with Him. As years passed, and I knew Jesus from a deeper, more mature perspective, I allowed Him access to the root of my pain, which brought a complete healing. Today the abuse is something I remember, but there isn't the slightest sting or ache; it's as though it happened to someone else and not to me.

We're complex beings. When the Lord puts His finger on a recurring issue, it's often because more healing is needed. Follow my analogy. To the left of the diagram (on the next page), is where the first abuse might have occurred.

At first there is acute pain, very real and present to you. Perhaps you weren't even a Christian at the time, but now as a Christian you've received counseling, or went into prayer and gave it to Jesus. You might have received deliverance from evil spirits that had exacerbated it.

Now years later a sermon is preached or a teacher touches on healing and the same issue arises. You question why the experience has resurfaced so intensely. The anguish is so strong that when you think of it, your physical heart aches. Some people say to ignore the inner voice; others say to rebuke it. Some who suffer these painful circumstances simply stay confused, thinking something is intrinsically wrong with them.

Here's my suggestion: Go ahead, let the Lord heal you at deeper levels each time the incident comes around. This isn't a lack of faith, but instead the Holy Spirit prompting you that there's more inner healing to be experienced. You will discover that over time the pain, the ache, and the reality of the abuse will fade away to nothing. Originally, at the core of the pillar event is severe agony.

Additional years later, the Holy Spirit stirs your heart about the same traumatic experience. But this time it's not nearly as painful. Do not be concerned with what others are thinking, but allow the Lord to go deeper in your life to root out any lingering unhealed areas.

Surprisingly, you might weep and weep at the altar. As someone prays for you, you sense a heaviness lifting from your head and shoulders. You don't understand exactly what happened, but you know God has again done something wonderful.

Unbelievably, five years later a conference about experiencing an intimate relationship with Jesus triggers the issue again. As you allow

Progressive Healing

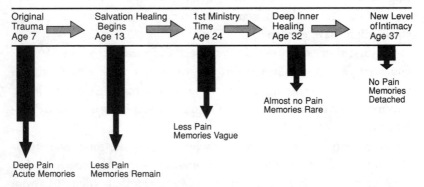

the Spirit to conduct divine surgery, this time He moves beyond your soul and into your spiritual core. In prayer, without your understanding the process, the Lord sifts all the way to the root of your original traumatic experience and pulls the last stinger from your heart.

Still visualizing the diagram, what was at one time a situation that brought you pain, fear, and torment is now little more than a memory. Because the Lord has healed you so completely, there isn't any pain. Although healing can come instantly, in one moment, the Spirit sometimes will have us address painful issues over a season of time.

For one thing, as new Christians we may be unable to capture the depth and breadth of God's ability to heal our deepest hurts, because we don't know His ways until we've walked many years together in fellowship.

Furthermore, God allows these "ouches" to resurface because often we've been taught to tough it out and to ignore the lingering pain. Where revelation is received, more revelation is given. If you are willing to obey the revelation the Lord gives you, He will give more. Our loving heavenly Father will wait for you and me to know Him. At first you may not have known who you were in Christ, but as your love for Him deepens, deeper cleansing and healing will follow.

LINKS

We've considered how impressions affect our beliefs and how reoccurrences of those impressions affect our behavior. Memory uses *associations,* which are links in the thought chain that attach one memory, good or bad, to another. For example, whenever there's a hurricane threat, my memory of Hurricane Carla in 1961 is triggered. I remember how we evacuated our home and stayed at Landa Park in New Braunfels, Texas, during the killer storm. The night the Texas Coast was hit, a brisk wind was blowing as my brother John and I swam in the park's spring-fed pool.

Understanding how these links work within the mind helps us see how the Holy Spirit heals our memories. Maybe every time you smell pot roast you remember the day your father left your mother. Or a certain street reminds you of childhood visits to your grandparents' house. Our memory will record the emotions we had while attending an unexpected funeral or about the thrill of hitting a game-winning homer.

So which emotions are triggered by your memories of victimization? What other memories are associated with (linked to) them? Our personalities differ. What would be a traumatic experience for one might not be traumatic for another. The difference lies in our emotional reactions.

I was popular in the seventh grade, and in the fall of that year some of my friends played a trick on me. They told me that the Friday night junior high dance at the city recreation hall was a costume party and everyone was to dress accordingly. Another friend and I did—I was a ballerina, and I don't recall what Janis wore. When we walked into the crowded room that night, we were the *only* ones in costumes. Everyone began to laugh and then broke into applause. I laughed too, and I bowed as they applauded, but Janis was devastated. Her reaction, the complete opposite of mine, was fear and humiliation.

Two completely different reactions. In the latter case, if a link is retained in our mind, eventually a memory of ridicule and embarrassment is formed as a negative association with those classmates. The associated connection makes it likely that the next time the person experiences a related or associated link to the past embarrassment, the same emotions will subconsciously reemerge. If fun and laughter was the original response, then fun and laughter will surface again; if fear and anxiety occurred, there will probably be a recurrence of the same.

The tendency of the mind to become programmed to react with certain repeated responses is the essence of a stronghold. If the person willingly believes lies from false or distorted memories, he or she may at some point open the door to demonic spirits.

I counseled with a Canadian pastor's wife who suffered from anxiety attacks. In reality, there was nothing for which she needed to be anxious, but she was nonetheless. Camille (not her real name) was too fearful to drive. She wouldn't be alone for fear someone would break into her house. She wouldn't leave home after dark for fear someone would attack her. I learned that Camille experienced abandonment by her father as a child. She was always insecure and nervous, and she mentally entertained lies about her well-being. These meditations of her heart were not of God.

Years ago, driving down the street in the middle of the day, Camille was suddenly convinced that her husband, Bob, on a long international missions trip, was going to die. At that time he was aboard a plane, so she couldn't contact him. She began to imagine what it would be like to raise their son on her own. She visualized the funeral, the grave, the loss of finances.

Like wildfire these thoughts raged through her mind for *years* afterward. Even though Bob had returned fine, Camille had linked her father's abandonment to the absence of her husband. This renewed her covenant with darkness and perpetuated her fear, anxiety, and inability to live a full life.

The emotions experienced during the link or pillar event (original trauma) will continue to be activated by associated experiences as long as a person allows it. When faced and dealt with decisively, the associative link is broken, shutting down those emotional responses to the past. As I prayed for Camille, she identified the pillar event of abandonment, and her healing came when the Spirit opened her eyes to the fear she'd experienced as a little girl. She acknowledged living as though God didn't care. Once she repented and renounced the lies, the demon that had been holding her left—there was now nothing for it to hold.

VICTIMIZATION SELF-EVALUATION

The graph below represents a scale of victimization. The numbers on the extreme left represent someone living under a victim mentality.

The numbers on the extreme right represent one who's broken free from victim cycles and is empowered to live and serve God as a life-giving believer. This scale is designed to help you graph where you are now and enable you to set some goals for the future.

VICTIMIZATION SELF-EVALUATION

(Circle the number above the line that most closely reflects the truth about you in each instance.)

(1) My Boundaries

1 2 3	4 5 6 7	8 9 10
I allow people to treat me as they please, even if it hurts. I never say anything.	I'm alert, and I maintain my personal boundaries. I recognize when I'm being disrespected or being disrespectful of others.	I experience quality communication with others. I expect others not to violate my boundaries. Others treat me with respect, and I treat others respectfully.

(2) Passivity

1 2 3	4 5 6 7	8 9 10
Yelling at others or being yelled at is normal to me. I make allowances for profanity (mine and/or others'). I'd rather keep my mouth shut and not make waves.	I rarely lift my voice in anger or resort to profanity. I respectfully correct those who do. I'm not willing to sit idly by and tolerate evil.	I don't suffer from guilt or false guilt. I keep my sins confessed, and I disregard the accusations of others or of the devil.

(3) Abuse

1	2	3	4	5	6	7	8	9	10
I endure abuses and tend to protect predators, abusers of others and me. Abusers seek and find me.			I'm able to stand my ground and don't keep silent when I or anyone else is being abused.				I'm able to receive and even expect protection from others, and I'm willing to protect others. I'm not a victim.		

(4) Deception

1	2	3	4	5	6	7	8	9	10
I'm used to lies; I think they're normal, and I even lie to myself. The devil takes advantage of me.			I can see the pain in other's lives, and I can run interference for them.				I walk in authority, and I freely walk in the truth. Others see integrity and transparency in me.		

(5) Dishonor

1	2	3	4	5	6	7	8	9	10
I attract abuse and dishonor. I don't say or do anything to stop it.			I talk badly about myself, but I won't allow others to talk badly about me.				Honor flows naturally to me, without my seeking it, in both formal and informal settings.		

(6) Ministry

1	2	3	4	5	6	7	8	9	10
I'm ineffective in ministry; I don't even try.			I can minister at surface levels when the conditions are right, but I am still very insecure in doing so.				I passionately pursue ministry, and ministry opportunities come to me. God blesses others when I minister.		

(7) Values

1	2	3	4	5	6	7	8	9	10
I don't have godly values and don't know how to set any. Almost anything goes.			I have godly values, but others don't always see them in me. If others are around who are stronger than me, I compromise my values to fit in.				I influence the values of others and see change in their lives.		

(8) Joy

1	2	3	4	5	6	7	8	9	10
I never experience joy; sadness is all I feel. Life is hard and cruel.			I have times of joy as well as times of discouragement. Every month it becomes easier to rejoice in times of trouble.				I leave a trail of joy for others to enjoy. My life is full and complete in God.		

(9) Potential

1	2	3	4	5	6	7	8	9	10
I allow and sometimes even enable others to abuse me; I don't see my kingdom potential (or even perceive that I have one).			I'm beginning to acknowledge who I am in Christ and to assume my kingdom responsibilities. I like what's changing in me.				I know God's plan for my life, and I actively live it. Doors regularly open for me to share my life with others.		

(10) Power

1	2	3	4	5	6	7	8	9	10
I feel that I'm powerless and unable to change my circumstances. The same cycle repeats itself again and again.			God is in the process of setting me free. I see glimpses of supernatural authority in me.				Even Christian leaders look to me for solutions. I know the Word; I am a person of prayer and feel God's anointing.		

(11) Curses and Blessings

1	2	3	4	5	6	7	8	9	10
Curses and troubles seem to follow me. Poverty is all I know.			Curses are beginning to be broken as I submit to God. I'm setting boundaries that prevent the devil from accusing me.				I freely receive God's blessings, financially, spiritually, and emotionally. I'm able to break curses that others are troubled by.		

Scoring:

To determine your score, total the numbers you've circled and divide them by 11.

GRADES:

70+ — No Victim Here!

40–69 — Beginning to overcome

11–39 — In a survival mode; needs attention

CHAPTER NINE:
Self-Talk: The Image Factor

Every waking moment people talk to themselves. Surprised? Did you think you were the only one? The question isn't *"Do* you talk to yourself?" but *"What* are you telling yourself?" Do you feed yourself the truth, or are you fooling yourself?

I have a close girl friend who *audibly* talks to herself, all the time. When I took a prayer team to Egypt some years ago, she roomed with me, and every morning while putting on makeup she giggled and chattered. I said, "You don't need our conversation—you're having fun all by yourself!"

Psychologists tell us that the average person speaks forty to fifty thousand things to her/himself daily, *70 percent or more of which are negative.* However, the most exceptional professional athletes are said to reduce their self-talk to twenty thousand or fewer statements, and less than 50 percent are negative: Focused positive thinking and self-talk are critical if you are to move from victimization to victory. Why? Because "faith cometh by hearing" (Romans 10:17). Your belief system is built on what you think *and* what you say to yourself, and not just on what you say aloud!

If TV commercials and other forms of repetitive advertisement weren't effective in selling products, no one would pay (much less pay a great amount) for them. Ask yourself, "What am I continually advertising and selling to my subconscious mind (my inner person) via self-talk?" Your subconscious has no power of judgment; it simply records data and experiences as they happen and then believes as true what it's told. Abuse, specifically, is part of a negative marketing campaign the devil designed to sell you on your personal failure.

This is why the words of your mouth (what you say to others), the meditations of your heart (what you say to yourself), and the words of others (who you listen to), whether positive or negative, greatly determine what you think, what you do, and who you'll eventually become. *Your self-talk should always be acceptable in God's sight.*

You're never unemployed: You'll always have the job of being your mind's gatekeeper. *You* determine what you'll allow yourself to see, to hear, and to think. *You're* the one who must learn God's Word if you intend to challenge and capture any thought contrary to His will and bring it into line with truth (2 Corinthians 10:4–5).

God holds you personally accountable for the temple He's given you to care for. So avoid negative friends and companions. Filter the movies you see, the music you hear, the downloads you watch, the magazines and books you read.

THE EFFECTS OF ATTITUDE

It's been said, "Your attitude determines your altitude." Your attitude definitely affects your relationships with God and others, and it unquestionably affects your own health—mental, emotional, and even physical. Possibly nothing can adversely affect your *attitude* in the same way as does abuse.

Abused people often struggle with forgiving their abuser, themselves, and even God. The negative nature of thoughts, feelings of unforgiveness, and bitterness sometimes produces physical illness and disease—remember, those might be understandable responses, but they're unacceptable for us. When Paul taught us to observe the Lord's Supper, he said that sin could cause sickness and even death (see 1 Corinthians 11:27–32).

Perhaps one reason your attitude can cause sickness, disease, and other forms of torment is that it also determines the level of your stress. Some people "stuff" their stress, quietly bearing it while others "shout" their stress, outwardly venting it. In either case, stress is a killer that accelerates and intensifies when our focus is anywhere other than where it needs to be. *The Message* paraphrase of Proverbs 3:5–8 says:

Trust GOD from the bottom of your heart;
don't try to figure out everything on your own.
Listen for GOD's voice in everything you do, everywhere you go;
he's the one who will keep you on track.
Don't assume that you know it all.
Run to GOD! Run from evil!
Your body will glow with health,
your very bones will vibrate with life!

If you choose to live a glass-half-empty life, you are doomed to disillusionment. The natural law of attraction guarantees it. You find in life what you're looking for, not what you're looking at. No doubt you attract what you are! If your perspective on life, including your past, is miserable, you will stay miserable. It's all about your perception.

- Ten percent of what makes you who you are is what's happened to you.
- Ninety percent of what makes you who you are is how you've chosen to respond to what's happened to you.

If you add to an unhealed past a bad attitude, the common pressures of everyday life, blue Mondays, parenting difficulties, and/or bumper-to-bumper traffic, you can be driven to despair. And never forget that demonic spirits work overtime to assure it.

Victims of abuse have negative emotions regarding their abusers, but the most complex and difficult problem to solve is their feelings concerning themselves—feelings that often have no basis in fact. If you continue to respond to life's ups and downs according to your past experiences rather than allowing the Holy Spirit to direct your responses, you will only strengthen any negative stronghold within.

Victims often harbor feelings ranging from disappointment and anger to hatred and rage toward their abusers. Rage is unrestrained anger combined with fear (anger out of control). Scripture teaches us to abhor anything evil; *rage is wrong*. Healing begins when one can differentiate between the act and the actor—it is possible to hate what was done and not hate the doer. In fact, we're taught not even to let the sun go down on our wrath, because when we let anger simmer overnight, we give place to the enemy.

JUSTICE IS REQUIRED

Resentment is reserving the right to re-feel one's anger. In effect, it's reserving the right to punish the perpetrator. Nevertheless, it's normal rather than simply vindictive for you to want to see your abuser punished. Why?

You want to see your abuser punished because God made you in His image. That's right. In His perfect holiness, God can't consider evil. He says, "The soul that sinneth, it shall die," and "the wages of sin is death" (Ezekiel 18:4; Romans 6:23). Justice flows out of God's very essence; you reflect His nature with your inner cries for righteousness and for justice against wrong. God's justice is programmed in you. Your heart demands it. The problem comes when you begin to believe that it's *your* prerogative rather than *God's* to be judge.

The key to forgiveness is recognizing that *the punishment you seek and that the abuser deserves has already been meted out.* When Jesus was nailed to the cross, He bore the sins of the world. He was punished for your sins and for the sins committed against you. When you see this and by faith accept that the sin debt owed to you has been paid in full by Christ's sacrifice, you will be able to lay down the desire for vengeance: Vengeance belongs to God alone (Romans 12:19). *God* has settled the matter so that you can have a heart free from bitterness, unforgiveness, rage, and retribution.

Relating to God

Victimization is devastating to a person's relationship with God. Scripture presents Father God to us as a protector (a trait of masculinity), whom we should trust to shield us. When we suffer abuse, especially at the hands of a male, we naturally feel that God has failed us. The emotional confusion stemming from abuse can cause us to respond to people and circumstances without hearing from and obeying God.

Because this hinders our ability to trust Him, it certainly affects our ability for spiritual intimacy in the place of prayer. We were born for spiritual intimacy with the Lord—this is our highest calling and purpose in life.

Relating to Others

Our relationship with others directly impacts our relationship with God. His Word makes this probing statement: "Anyone who does not love his brother, whom he has seen, cannot love God, whom he has not seen" (1 John 4:20 NIV).

Commonly, one who's been abused becomes prideful to compensate for feelings of inadequacy. A drivenness toward rebuilding lost self-esteem can be a way to escape the memories and in some cases to compensate for one's feelings of worthlessness. The result of pride is . . . a fall (Proverbs 16:18).

This too can become a life cycle. After a fall, we feel failure, and we're prone to compensate by covering failure with more pride. And, again, pride comes before a fall. When we feel badly about ourselves, we're likely to shift the attention off our failures and to identify— even magnify—the faults of others. This traces all the way back to the fall of mankind (Genesis 3).

Comparing ourselves with others is easy—we can always find someone who's "worse" than we are. Ironically, such comparisons make us feel better about ourselves temporarily because the focus is shifted from our inadequacy to someone else's. But it's unwise to do so; *God,* and God alone, is the standard for us in every way (2 Corinthians 10:17–18).

Relating to Self

Abuse hinders our ability to recognize, receive, and experience true love. When those we love, those who should have loved us, elevate themselves and their needs above ours, we're left confused. How can abuse and love coexist? (See 1 Corinthians 13.)

Some young people marry the wrong person—or the right person at the wrong time—because they're confused about true love. Because judgmental people find it hard to believe they could possibly be truly loved, they (often subconsciously) push away true love because of perceived feelings of unworthiness. If you've suffered abuse, ask yourself the following questions:

- Do I constantly question the love of others?
- Do I tend to question the motives, sincerity, and intentions of others and ask, "What do they want from me?"
- Do I do this subconsciously to the point where they feel rejection from me?
- Do they sense this because of my subtle behaviors and body language?

This is how the rejection cycle normally works:

- We are rejected (or abused) by someone we love and from whom we expected to receive love.
- In turn we reject those who really do love and care about us.
- This results in cyclically attracting abusive people.

Our response severely compromises our ability both to experience and to express true love. What we don't recognize, we can't receive. What we can't receive, we'll never experience. What we've not experienced, we can't express. And without a miracle of inner healing, the cycle continues.

Don't set your focus on building self-esteem. Esteeming yourself is no more scriptural than despising yourself (see 2 Timothy 3:2). It isn't self-esteem you need, it's self-respect and self-acceptance. If you don't accept yourself as a child of God and respect the gift that He made you to be, you're not only sinning against yourself, but you are actually judging God's handiwork.

Creator God formed you from conception! Psalm 139:13–14 says:

Oh yes, you shaped me first inside, then out;
you formed me in my mother's womb.
I thank you, High God—you're breathtaking!
Body and soul, I am marvelously made!
I worship in adoration—what a creation! (THE MESSAGE).

To move from victim to victor, you must once and for all be free from the embarrassment, shame, guilt (even false guilt), and reproach of your past. That's the wonderful result of a person who knows who he is, who sees why God has made him, and who accepts and appreciates who he is. This isn't self-esteem, it's self-acceptance—becoming a good steward of one's self.

GOD LOVES US BECAUSE
HE WANTS TO LOVE US

What causes us to succumb to self-rejection? Is it because of what others have done to us? Is it because of what we've chosen to believe about ourselves?

We must clarify one important truth: *God loves us just as we are.* He loves us when we do right and when we do wrong; our sin doesn't affect His love for us. His love is truly unconditional—He loves us under every condition of life. We may grieve His heart, but we can never escape His love.

"God is love" (1 John 4:8) and love is His very nature. That's why even while we were bound to sin, God showed His love for us in Christ's death for us (Romans 5:8). The Lord loved us when we were His enemy, and there's nothing that can separate us from His love for all eternity. Hallelujah!

Accordingly, our self-respect and self-acceptance should be based on His awesome love, not our works. Our self-worth (the value we place on ourselves) should be based on His having created us for His own purpose. God has programmed into each of us a kingdom potential, a life-assignment that only we can accomplish.

You might protest, "But what about the weakness I feel? What about my flaws? What about how I look, what I can't achieve, my education or lack of it?" Certainly some of those things are our responsibility—some we can and should change, and self-improvement is always in order. Even so, there are things we can't change, and those we simply accept as we release them to God. Paul wrote, "Godliness with contentment is great gain" (1 Timothy 6:6).

Being strong isn't the ultimate goal—being His *is* ! When we belong to the Lord and rely on Him in obedience, He will demonstrate His strength through our weaknesses. He chooses the foolish things to confound the world's "wise" (1 Corinthians 1:27), and in this way He receives the greatest glory.

The question isn't about your ability or inability but about your *availability*. It's possible that as you've sought to understand and make sense of the abuses and the betrayals you've suffered, you've actually judged God too. If that's the case, I am praying that this truth will till the soil of your heart and cause you to repent for calling into question the integrity of your precious, perfect heavenly Father.

Perhaps (like me) you have asked, "Why didn't God stop the abuse and betrayal I experienced? Where was He when all of this was happening? How could He stand by and let it take place? Why didn't He stop the perpetrator of my pain? Why did He allow this?"

Though these are perfectly reasonable questions, we'll never know the full reasons during this lifetime. God reserves certain things to himself. At the same time, there are a few things of which we can be certain: God was grieved when you were grieved. He suffered when you suffered. He was hurting when you were hurting.

God is self-restricted by the law of His own nature. He created us not as robots but as moral agents with the ability to make decisions—

love is so priceless that it's worth the freedom it affords. God mysteriously allows sin to run its course until we are convinced that mankind is utterly incapable of righteousness apart from Christ.

God protected me and sustained my life. As with Job, He didn't allow Satan to destroy me. *That's* why I'm still here. *That's* why I survived. More important, *that* is why I can be more than a conqueror through Christ! And that's why I write this to you—the joy I experience today can be yours also.

One day a young father heard his elementary-age son screaming hysterically in the backyard. A bee was buzzing around the child's head and he was racing in circles, arms flailing, trying to escape its sting.

The father called for his son to stop running and be still. After several tense moments, the boy obeyed his father. When the bee finally buzzed away, he rushed to his father's side.

"Son," the father said, "look at my arm. What do you see?" The one stinger the bee had was lodged deeply there. "Son, the bee already used its stinger. It couldn't harm you, except to make you run into something and hurt yourself out of fear."

Two thousand years ago, Jesus took out Satan's stinger at Calvary, disarming him completely. The devil can only hurt you now if you choose to embrace fear and believe what isn't true.

Once my hurtful past was reconciled to God's plan and I had its "stinger" removed, it became a positive part of my new life. The abuse I suffered is no longer a liability. My God has moved it from the debit column to the credit column. The pain of the old things died, and the old things became new (see 2 Corinthians 5:17). Remember, the memories don't cease to exist, they simply no longer provoke pain. Best of all, they take on new potential: It's common for those who have suffered abuse to become counselors and ministers to others! God will use what were once your areas of great weakness to bring glory to His magnificent strength.

You will no longer have to run from, hide from, or deny your past—you can allow Christ to reconcile and redeem it. You reach emotional maturity as you discover and internalize God's truth. It's often said that after twenty-one days of repeating the same behavior a habit is formed. Engage in activities that will lead to new, productive habits facilitating your restoration.

Begin to reprogram your mind with truths!

- Start today, not tomorrow.
  - Act decisively. Initiate action; don't just respond.
    - Tune in and become friends with emotionally healthy people.
      - Walk away from the 90 percent who don't want to be happy and join the 10 percent who do.
        - You only have time for one passion in life.
          - Choose your passion and go forward!

CHAPTER TEN:
Establishing Your New Identity

I love Darrell Evans' popular song:

I'm trading my sorrow,
I'm trading my shame,
I'm laying it down for the joy of the Lord.

I'm trading my sickness,
I'm trading my pain,
I'm laying it down for the joy of the Lord.

And we say yes, Lord, yes, Lord, yes, yes, Lord . . . Amen.[1]

Reconciliation with others and with ourselves is critical, but these are impossible if we ignore our relationship with God. The answer begins with *"Christ in you,"* which is, as the apostle Paul wrote, "the hope of glory" (Colossians 1:27). We will glorify the Lord with our lives when Christ comes to live His triumphant, victorious life in us!

Flour, salt, milk, shortening, baking powder. If you're a cook, you might recognize these items as the ingredients for biscuits. Well, God has given us all the ingredients for a fulfilling life (2 Peter 1:3), for with Christ in us, we possess all things needful for living righteously and freely in Him. But knowing the ingredients isn't enough—we must also have the recipe. For instance, if you knead the dough too long the biscuits will be hard once they're baked. The ingredients are the *means;* the recipe enables you to achieve a successful *result.*

THE RECIPE FOR FREEDOM

(1) Stop Procrastinating and Making Excuses.

Thanks be unto God, which always causeth us to triumph in Christ, and maketh manifest the savour of his knowledge by us in every place. (2 Corinthians 2:14)

Many years ago while in prayer, the Lord said, "Alice, you can have as much of me as you want." I made the decision to stop making excuses for areas of my life that needed transformation.

During recovery from surgery, listening to an Arthur Burk tape on setting boundaries, I heard, "You'll never fulfill your kingdom purpose as long as you continue to live as a victim." Immediately I realized I needed to stop making excuses for not fully acknowledging the open doors God had given me, and begin to move forward toward my destiny without intimidation. I repented for allowing people to dishonor and disrespect me. I told the Lord I wouldn't permit it to continue—I would take the initiative and set boundaries. It wasn't an issue of pride; it was accepting my responsibility to set healthy boundaries that determines how I allow myself to be treated.

Not long after, as a speaker I began to notice that when times of ministry came, instead of backing away from assignments, I stepped up. When I was around an influential person and felt the Lord had given me a key to help in some area, I would confidently offer it. The tables had turned. Before long such people began to ask for my help. Today the boundaries of my life are secure, and God is enlarging them. Thankfully, I'm able to walk in His authority as favor goes before me. (Thank you, Jesus!) This could not have happened had I continued to make excuses.

(2) Ask God to Reveal the Pillar Events (Root Issues).

[I pray that] the eyes of your understanding [will be] enlightened; that ye may know what is the hope of his calling, and what [are] the riches of the glory of his inheritance in the saints. (Ephesians 1:18)

Sit quietly before the Lord and ask Him to reveal the pillar events, the life experiences that have compelled you to live as a victim. The Holy Spirit is the Spirit that discloses; allow Him time to show you. You'll know it's the Lord as an image comes to mind or as He speaks something to your heart. It won't be condemning, but it may be convicting—the Spirit works from the inside out, while the devil works from the outside in.

The enemy condemns and harasses with general accusations, speaking in generalities like "You're a lousy Christian." God will not leave you confused. He convicts us of specific offenses, and with Him we know without a doubt of what we should repent. Even if His words break our hearts, we will realize a new tenderness toward Him and others.

Ask for God's revelation of pillar events in two areas.

- **Points of Trauma:** First, ask the Lord to reveal points of trauma, terror, abuse, et al. Don't fabricate. If the event was real, you'll remember it. One by one, repent for any unforgiveness, resentment, hatred, bitter root, or hostility you've held toward anyone—family, friend, or foe. Release each person to God. *You will not receive any further breakthrough if you insist on clinging to your offense.*

- **Personal Sins:** Second, make a list of sins you've committed. These may or may not be sins for which you've repented; *beyond* repentance, you're making this list to break the enemy's hold on your life. Rick Warren, pastor and bestselling author of *The Purpose Driven Life,* speaks this way about freedom from the past:

    You've undoubtedly heard the expression "Time heals all wounds." Unfortunately, it isn't true. As a pastor I frequently talk with people who still carry hurts from 30 or 40 years ago. The truth is, time often makes things worse. Wounds left untended fester and spread infection throughout your entire body. Time only extends the pain if the problem isn't dealt with.[2]

(3) Repent of the Lies and Believe the Truth.

If we say that we have fellowship with him, and walk in darkness, we lie, and do not the truth. (1 John 1:6)

Salvation is a person, not just an experience. Your salvation is sealed and guaranteed when Christ comes to live in you. He guarantees your eternal security (heaven); He provides the power and resources you need to face earthly responsibilities; and He reconciles your painful, sinful past. Christ in you buffers, resolves, and heals you from abuses suffered at the hands of others.

Because you're an entirely new creature, your hurtful earthly past (the history of your old life) doesn't have the right to dictate to you anymore. You are neither a victim nor a mere survivor—Christ has made you an overcomer! Respect and receive yourself as a gift from God with kingdom purpose. Do this right now. Tell the Lord, "I respect myself, Jesus. You have made me to be your handiwork, and I accept myself just as I am. In your name. Amen."

Put off false guilt today. We've all suffered some form of abuse. Even Christ was abused, yet the devil never had a place in Him. Paul told Timothy, "If we suffer, we shall also reign with him" (2 Timothy 2:12). Jesus has redeemed you entirely, which includes the abuses you've suffered. Rise above the past, and let others see God's glory through you.

If you've been living your life as a victim and not a victor, you've believed lies. They may be lies about you, lies about others, and/or lies about the devil. But the most debilitating are the lies you've believed about God and His love. Ask Him to reveal these to you, and then list them. Ask yourself . . .

- Have I doubted God's love for me?
- Have I doubted God's ability to protect me?
- Have I doubted God's forgiveness—His cleansing?
- Have I questioned God's purpose for my life?
- Have I believed my "self-righteousness" is the basis of my salvation?
- Have I believed I could never overcome?
- What else?

(4) Break Unholy Soul Ties.

His own iniquities shall take the wicked himself, and he shall be holden with the cords of his sins. (Proverbs 5:22)

Next, it's important that you break the unholy soul ties with those who've participated in your sin or those who've abused you. An unholy soul tie is like a spiritual cord of sin that joins people together. Your common sin with someone is part of the fabric, the very identity of that relationship. As such, it is a limiting factor in your spiritual freedom and growth, keeping you in permanent bondage until you confess aloud and break the contracts that relate to it.

A godly union between husband and wife can bring blessing and joy to their relationship, but an unholy union (through rape, incest, fornication, adultery, pornography, predator partnership, bestiality, homosexuality, lesbianism) may establish a spiritual cord of iniquity that provides opportunity for demonic transfer between the iniquitous partners.

Pray to Jesus:

Lord, I love you, and I never want to dishonor you. Your truth is setting me free. Continue the revelation of all the unholy soul ties made between another and me, both physically and emotionally. I am sorry for the wrong relationships I have partnered in, and I turn from them now. Cleanse me and set me free from any hold the enemy has on me. Please show me any object from a wrong relationship that I need to discard, and I will obey you, Lord, by getting rid of it. In your wonderful name. Amen.

(5) Break Contracts With Darkness.

Ye have not received the spirit of bondage again to fear; but ye have received the Spirit of adoption, whereby we cry, Abba, Father. (Romans 8:15)

Say aloud, with your eyes open,

Spirits of darkness, I break any and all unholy soul ties between me and _____ (say the name of the person); I cancel all sexual transference in the powerful name of Jesus Christ. I cancel any control or manipulation between me and _____. And I refuse and break any and all ungodly soul ties between family members and me, through vows, ceremonies, rituals, secrets, contracts, or alliances. All ties to the demonic are broken now. Heeding the words of Matthew 3:10, I lay an axe to any unfruitful root of darkness, whether past or present. Your hold on me is over NOW.

(6) Establish Healthy Boundaries.

LORD, you have assigned me my portion and my cup; you have made my lot secure. The boundary lines have fallen for me in pleasant places; surely I have a delightful inheritance. (Psalm 16:5–6 NIV)

I want to be extremely clear concerning this step. I'm not endorsing arrogance, a pushy attitude, or demanding your rights. I'm saying that too often we don't have thought-out, in-place boundaries that protect us from the intentions of evil people, demons, or sometimes just controlling individuals. We can have established boundaries that protect us from manipulation or control *and* still demonstrate humility, compassion, honesty, integrity, purity, and gentleness (see Ephesians 4:32; Colossians 3:12–14).

Although they hated Him, Jesus didn't allow the Sadducees or Pharisees to victimize or control Him. When it came to their arrogance and pride, He responded, "O generation of vipers, how can ye, being evil, speak good things? for out of the abundance of the heart the mouth speaketh" (Matthew 12:34). Jesus knew their thoughts and their hearts; He recognized the need to maintain godly boundaries so evil men would not take advantage of Him. We must do the same;

however, we need to examine our heart to ensure that our responses are coming from the Lord rather than out of our soul that might be wounded.

Offenders will continue to invade your space if you allow them to. Don't! And don't go to places where you're likely to be victimized. Guard your own behavior, and assume responsibility for how you allow people to treat you. Enforce your freedom from past victimization and watch that you don't fall into the same cycle. You can't continue doing the same things you've done for years and expect different results.

How can you change your patterns of thinking and speaking?

(1) Decide right now how you'll allow people to treat you, then stand tall.
(2) Become aware of how you previously allowed people to manipulate and control you.
(3) Square your shoulders and don't slump; carry yourself with dignity.
(4) Shake hands firmly and with confidence.
(5) Dress appropriately, maintaining a finished look with clean hair and nails. You don't have to be wealthy to present yourself nicely.
(6) Learn the skill of establishing and upholding boundaries during encounters. Prepare ahead how you might answer or react.
(7) Look people directly in the eyes when you speak with them.
(8) Speak clearly and precisely. Don't mumble or stutter.
(9) If it would be easier for you, find a faithful friend with whom you can practice these guidelines.

Learn to discern each situation. The moment you identify a manipulative "power play," with a calm and gentle voice tell the abusive person that you won't tolerate condescending or demeaning treatment. Sometimes a critical or condemning person with whom you're interacting is simply having a bad day. In this case, encourage the person with kind words. If the person is exhibiting bad manners, model good manners in front of him or her.

Sometimes, though, the person is a pawn of the devil to intimidate you into an abusive cycle. In that case, gently call that person into question. Don't raise your voice or react wildly; doing so means you've engaged in the power struggle, which is what your antagonist wants from you.

Example: You were fortunate to have Christian parents growing up. However, your entire life you've borne the guilt trips your mother puts on you. Even though you're an adult with three growing children of your own, if there's anything your mother wants done (*right now*), regardless of your schedule, you're the one she calls.

You jump at her every word. If you can't do what she requires, she accuses you of being selfish and unconcerned. She berates you with the Bible, sermonizing about children obeying their parents. Not measuring up to her expectations has driven you to fulfill her every desire. You allow her to abuse you emotionally and verbally.

Children *are* to obey their parents—in Ephesians 6, the word *obey* means "be subordinate to." As children we're subordinate to our parents; as adults, when we married or moved away, we left our mother and father and took on a new role. Respecting and honoring your parents—always. Listening to and seeking their advice—you bet. Always doing what they say . . . not necessarily. Many fine believers are tormented by controlling and abusive parents who manipulate them with "religious words." There's a fine balance between honoring and having an unhealthy relationship. Make sure you kindly express your willingness to serve, love, and help in any way possible, but also make it clear you won't be manipulated or placed into an unhealthy role.

Some years ago I spoke at Peter Wagner's conference in St. Louis. The message I brought was a new one for me, but one that had been stirring in my heart for months. Once I gave the invitation, the altars were filled with repentant, tearful people. God did amazing things in many lives that day.

I was still at the altar when a pastor approached me arrogantly and said, "Alice, that was an anointed message. I wish I had delivered it. But why would God use a woman to deliver it instead of a man? He wouldn't!"

I looked him straight in the eye, smiled, and softly answered, "Pastor, your words are entirely inappropriate. God is my defense. You take the matter up with Him."

Once he realized that I wouldn't cower, cry, or be humiliated, he turned around and walked away. Not that I needed his apology, but there was once a time when I allowed people to speak rude, cynical, and hurtful words to me without challenge. No longer. You too can learn to stand your ground, challenge injustice, and if necessary, suffer for righteousness' sake.

(7) Toughen Up.

Be strong in the Lord, and in the power of his might. (Ephesians 6:10)

I always look forward to springtime in Houston, because around our neighborhood are vacant lots filled with thick bushes of blackberries. Last year was exceptional for plump, juicy berries. If you can endure the heat, the humidity, the possibility of snakes (my next-door neighbor was almost bitten once) and the pain of thorns pricking your purple-stained fingers, the experience is worth it. Those thorns *are* painful, but on the day I was picking berries the Spirit of God reminded me that my sore, stained fingers were nothing when compared to the enjoyment of watching my family gobble up homemade blackberry cobbler with Texas-favorite Blue Bell ice cream. That's the way it is with many things. The process can hurt, but the benefits are worth it.

When Jesus told Simon Peter that Satan desired to sift him as wheat, Peter was probably paralyzed with fear. Just imagine what you'd have thought if Jesus had told you that! Well, guess what? Satan does desire to sift you as wheat. Further, he already has, and he'll continue to sift you.

When Jesus said, "Peter, I've prayed for you," perhaps Peter sighed with relief, thinking, *Phew! I thought for a moment I* was *going to be sifted.* However, Jesus didn't pray that Peter wouldn't be sifted—He prayed that the sifting of Peter would make him strong enough to strengthen others. And Jesus continues to pray the same for His people today (Hebrews 7:25).

Realistically, everyone will be sifted. Scripture clearly teaches that the rain falls on the just and the unjust (Matthew 5:45). Our blessing as Christians is that Satan's sifting need not destroy us; in fact, it's often the vehicle of our victory. What doesn't kill us does make us strong! King David said it this way: "Thou hast enlarged me when I was in distress" (Psalm 4:1). It isn't on the mountaintop that we're strengthened, but on the climb up from the bottom.

Shut down the pity party. Stop being a worrier and become a warrior. Stop whining and start winning. Trade your "new whine" for God's new wine. It's not what happens to you but how you respond to it that makes you *bitter* or *better.* Are you ready to stop wasting your sorrows and begin investing them in God's kingdom?

It's one thing to be sifted with God's permission for the purpose of your personal development; it's completely another for you to foolishly allow others to sift you for their ungodly power struggles. Nevertheless, *either* will be hard as long as you're overly concerned with what other people think about you. The Lord is the strength of your life. Toughen up!

(8) When You're Betrayed, Respond As Christ Did.

Jesus said unto him, "Friend, wherefore art thou come?" Then came they, and laid hands on Jesus, and took him. (Matthew 26:50)

Don't focus on your pain. When Judas betrayed Jesus, He didn't let His immediate pain distract Him from God's ultimate plan. Don't allow bitterness into your heart. Yes, it really is your choice. Don't let disappointments keep you from possible divine appointments! Jesus never lost sight of His calling, purpose, or ministry. When Peter slashed off the ear of the high priest's servant, Jesus continued to minister healing. Betrayal will be part of life. Allow it to be a stepping-stone to a new level of spiritual growth as you continue to serve, love, and forgive.

(9) Thank God for the Privilege of Being Tested.

Be not overcome of evil, but overcome evil with good. (Romans 12:21)

Testing teaches us God's unfailing faithfulness and sufficiency. We are to give thanks "in all things" (Ephesians 5:20). We are to celebrate, literally throw a party, when we're tested. James said,

My brethren, count (*hegeômai*—"command the lead") it all joy (*chara*—"sheer delight") when you fall (*peripiptô*—line up in a straight column) into divers (*poikilos*—"various kinds of") temptations (*peirasmos*—"putting to proof by experience of evil"). (James 1:2)

My paraphrase/amplification would be:

Brothers and sisters, command the front of the line with sheer delight in thanking God that you are chosen to be tested by various trials. They are proof that you can be joyful in the midst of evil. Trouble is your friend, not your enemy. Your trial is proof that God is gently, purposefully handling your life.

Trials deepen your relationship with the Lord, providing opportunities to develop an intimate connection with Jesus through prayer.

Adversities force you out of fleshly living and into Christ's lordship, qualifying you for ministry you'd otherwise not be able to offer. Like Peter, you too can strengthen others.

Remember Alka-Seltzer's zippy commercial that advertised relief from heartburn? "Plop, plop, fizz, fizz, oh, what a relief it is!" This may be a play on words, but I believe if you apply the advice of this chapter, you will experience spiritual relief.

Rick Warren offers the following eight principles for living a victorious life in Christ, an acronym for the word *RECOVERY.* To apply them daily, I suggest you read them aloud twice daily: first thing each morning and before retiring each evening. Here I've paraphrased them into declarations for you.[3]

R = Principle #1: Realize I'm Not God

I am powerless to control my tendency to do the wrong thing or to prevent my tendency toward sin. I am incapable of managing my life.

E = Principle #2: Earnestly Believe God Exists

I earnestly believe that God exists and that I matter to Him. He alone is the power of my recovery.

C = Principle #3: Consciously Commit

I commit my life, my possessions, and my relationships to Christ's care and control.

O = Principle #4: Openly Examine and Confess

I quickly repent and confess my sins to God. When I sin against anyone, I quickly repent and confess my sin to that person. Having done so, I instantly forgive myself, accepting Christ's forgiveness and claiming His righteousness.

V = Principle #5: Voluntarily Submit

I agree to every change God wants to make in my life, and I humbly ask Him to remove my character defects.

E = Principle #6: Evaluate All Relationships

I continually evaluate all the relationships in my life and agree to break off unhealthy or unholy associations. I forgive those who've hurt me or used me. I make amends for harm I've done to others, except when doing so would harm them or others.

R = Principle #7: Reserve a Daily Time With God

I set aside time each day to read my Bible and pray, to better know my heavenly Father and His will for my life. I will conduct self-examination only for the purpose of gaining spiritual power to follow His will.

Y = Principle #8: Yield to God

I yield myself to God right now. I will speak life to myself and to others, both by my example and by my words.

CHAPTER ELEVEN:
Kingdom Intimacy

The devil is a spoiler, determined to destroy your effectiveness as a Christian through life's traumatic experiences. He wants to keep you so victimized that the last thing on your mind will be to trust the Lord and develop an intimate prayer life. Satan presumes that bondage, shame, guilt, and disgrace will sidetrack you from wanting more of Jesus. It's left to you to prove him wrong.

From the beginning of time God has had something on His heart. He wants an intimate personal relationship with you . . . yes, you! As God fashioned a bride for Adam, He also had it in His heart to fashion a bride for His Son, Jesus. Central to God's heart is His desire to have covenant relationship with you. From this love have come many spiritual children. But to experience this fellowship, *you,* yourself, must hunger and thirst for Him.

King David, a man after God's own heart, wrote, "As the hart panteth after the water brooks, so panteth my soul after thee, O God" (Psalm 42:1). In this passage he paints a stunning portrait of what it means to thirst for the Lord.

On a hot, arid afternoon in the Near-Eastern Judean hills, the parched little hart nestles under bushy shrubs near a shimmering pool, waiting for sunset—for now, he's too overheated to move. As hours pass, his attention is focused only on water; nothing matters but quenching his thirst. Picture him in your mind: His eyes are transfixed. He audibly pants. Longing . . . waiting . . . and thirsting.

As soon as the sun disappears, the hart leaves his hiding place and dashes down the slope to lap up cool, refreshing water until he's completely refreshed.

David compares the hart's thirst for water to his thirst for his Lord: "O God, even as the hart longs and waits for the brook, I am yearning and thirsting for you" (paraphrase). Jesus Christ, our bridegroom, the heavenly Lover of our soul, seeks a spiritual bride who will pine after Him the same way. David *craved* God:

> O God, you are my God,
> earnestly I seek you;
> my soul thirsts for you,
> my body longs for you,
> in a dry and weary land
> where there is no water. (Psalm 63:1 NIV)

COVENANT RELATIONSHIP

The ancient Jewish custom of matrimony was different than our Western practices (though many Jewish customs are still honored in weddings today). Two thousand years ago a Jewish marriage was a legal matter established by covenant contract. When a young man saw a girl he desired (or when his parents had made a prior commitment), he would go to the girl's home with a contract containing all stipulations of the proposed marriage. He would work hard to offer the best dowry he could, because the most important part of the contract was what he was willing to offer the girl's father for permission to marry her.

The price of the bride was in one sense an expression of her worth; she wouldn't feel very valuable if the groom wasn't willing to sacrifice to marry her. Once the hopeful suitor offered the written covenant, the girl and her father would consider the proposal. If the terms were suitable, the young man and woman would drink a glass of wine together to seal the agreement. Before the groom departed from his future bride's home, he left a message for her: "I go to prepare a place for you."

Now the real work began, for the groom's responsibility was to build a beautiful bridal chamber for the upcoming wedding. This required an understanding of the bride's likes and dislikes, and it was crucial that the groom adorned the chamber with everything that would bless and please his new bride. This was no short-term project. It would often take as much as a year to complete. He didn't get off easy either, for after he was finished, the groom's father would inspect the room to see if it was suitable.

During the time of waiting the bride was preparing herself: sewing her dress, readying her clothes, grooming her hair and nails. A significant duty was to keep her lamp filled with oil in the event her groom came for her at night. Her bridesmaids were to prepare their lamps as well; they must be ready and waiting with expectancy toward that great day. During this time, friends in the community referred to the prospective bride as "consecrated," or "bought with a price," which meant she was unavailable to other young men.

After the bridal chamber was built and decorated, at just the right time, the groom and his groomsmen would surprise the bride, approaching her house with a shout to alert her that the wedding was close at hand. The joyful bride gathered her bridesmaids, put on her garment, and grabbed her clothes for the honeymoon. The men would steal away the women, and off into the night they would go.

Their lamps lit the night, and shouts of joy filled the streets as the wedding party walked through town. No one would recognize the bride because she wore a veil over her face.

Upon arrival at the groom's home, the bride and groom entered the room alone and closed the door. The chamber was the place for passionate love, a place for secrets and disclosure. Meanwhile, outside the house, the groom's father gathered family and friends to celebrate the marriage commitment.

Inside the chamber the bride and groom consummated their union; by Jewish tradition, the marriage wasn't acknowledged until physical intimacy had occurred. (See Matthew 19:5–6, 1 Corinthians 6:16.) Occasionally the best man came to the door to listen for the groom's voice, and once the marriage was consummated, the groom would confirm the union to his friend. The best man would then announce the good news to the waiting group, and the celebration would begin.

This was a time to rejoice. Now a marriage feast fit for a king would be served in honor of the happy couple. At the end of the festivities, the married couple would leave his father's house and go to their own home. On the way, the community would recognize the bride, no longer wearing her veil.[1]

UNION WITH CHRIST

John the Baptist describes the heavenly marriage between us and Jesus. "The bride belongs to the bridegroom. The friend who attends the bridegroom waits and listens for him, and is full of joy when he hears the bridegroom's voice. That joy is mine, and it is now complete" (John 3:29 NIV).

Never think you are insignificant. We are the bride of Christ! Jesus, the Lover of your soul, offered His own life as the highest price to purchase you. As the sipping of wine sealed the Jewish marriage contract, Jesus symbolically sealed His covenant with us when He shared wine with His disciples at the Last Supper. Having been chosen, we are to be consistently consecrated, prepared, living our lives separated from other lovers, and devoted to Christ. Paul said, "I am jealous for you with a godly jealousy. I promised you to one husband, to Christ, so that I might present you as a pure virgin to him" (2 Corinthians 11:2 NIV).

You have a promise! Just as the groom left the bride's home to build her wedding chamber, Jesus, whispering His words of love into your heart, is now preparing a place for you:

> Let not your heart be troubled; you believe in God, believe also in Me. In My Father's house are many mansions; if it were not so, I would have told you. I go to prepare a place for you. And if I go and prepare a place for you, I will come again and receive you to Myself; that where I am, there you may be also. (John 14:1–3 NKJV)

The Jewish bride removed her veil once her marriage was consummated: "He brought me to the banqueting house, and his banner over me was love" (Song of Solomon 2:4). At the time of Jesus' death on the cross (see Matthew 27:51), the temple veil between the Holy Place and the Holy of Holies was torn from top to bottom, forever removing the separation between God and us.

First, in saving (justifying) us, Christ removes our veil. Then He invites us beyond the veil into God's presence, from which we were once forbidden because of our sin. Now, by His blood, we can go boldly into the throne room with confidence, sharing with Jesus our every need. His perfect sacrifice can eradicate our guilt and shame. We can experience fully the joy of this inexpressible love affair that the world will never understand.

But let's not stop here—it's crucial that we catch a glimpse of our destiny. *Kingdom intimacy is a spiritual bride (us) seeking the plan and purpose of her heavenly bridegroom.* The plan? That we will bear much fruit (see John 15). We are the bride who goes into the chamber of prayer, receives the burden of our bridegroom, and travails to see men, women, boys, and girls born again. Who better to do this than those who've experienced the lows of trauma and abuse? Having known the depths of rejection, we can pray empathetically and effectively for those who haven't yet found the meaning of eternal life.

Souls are the result of our intimacy with the King. Millions worldwide are languishing in darkness; they haven't experienced the joy of salvation! As you consummate your relationship with Jesus, Spirit to spirit, heart to heart, you will become "spiritually pregnant" with His passion.

The Lord Jesus is calling you into the bridal chamber of love. He destroys the yokes of bondage that have captured your attention. He purifies you from the pain and shame you have known. He puts His arms around you and softly whispers, "Come."

> The Spirit and the bride say, "Come!" And let him who hears say, "Come!" Whoever is thirsty, let him come; and whoever wishes, let him take the free gift of the water of life. (Revelation 22:17 NIV)

CHAPTER TWELVE:
My Prince Charming

Though you now know much of my story, I've left some of the best for the end of this book. Journey with me now to a place of childhood dreams. One of my favorite stories as a young girl was *Cinderella*, a tale that I see has several interesting parallels to our sacred marriage with Christ.

Once upon a time, though it was not in my time or in your time, or in anybody else's time, there was a great king who had an only son, the prince and heir who was about to come of age. So the king sent around a herald who should blow his trumpet at every four corners where two roads met. And when the people came together he would call out, "O yes, O yes, O yes, know ye that his grace the king will give on Monday sennight"—that meant seven nights or next week—"a royal ball to which all maidens of noble birth are hereby summoned; and be it furthermore known unto you that at this ball his highness the prince will select unto himself a lady that shall be his bride and our future queen. God save the king.

Father God has a Son, Jesus Christ, who paid the ultimate price to have a bride of His own. We have been given the charge to blow trumpets in declaration of the King's intention to find a bride for His Son. We are His witnesses!

Now there was a widower, *of the king's court,* who had a lovely daughter that he felt needed a mother to care for and protect her. The father soon married a woman with two evil, malicious daughters. Instead of caring for Cinderella, her new step-mom abused her. She gave her stepdaughter the castoff clothes of her darling children. The noble's sad daughter was to do all the drudgery of housecleaning, to attend the kitchen fire, and had to sleep on the heap of cinder, and that is why they called her *Cinderella*.

When they heard the king's proclamation by the herald, the greedy sisters said, "What shall we wear, mother; what shall we wear?" They all began talking about which dress should suit the one and what dress should suit the other. They also consulted Cinderella in the matters, for she had excellent ideas, and her advice was always good. Indeed, she even offered her services to fix their hair, which they very willingly accepted. As she was doing this, they said to her, "Cinderella, would you not like to go to the ball?"

"Alas!" said she, "you only tease me; it is not for someone like me to go to such a place."

"You are quite right," they replied. "People would laugh to see a cinder-wench like you at a ball."

Now when the night came for the royal ball, Cinderella helped the two sisters to dress in their fine clothes and saw them drive off in the carriage with her father and their mother. But she went to her own mother's grave and sat beneath the hazel tree and wept and cried out.

Often the world's whispering voices rejoice foolishly, never noticing the tears of those rejected. Not only did Cinderella have to gracefully endure the callous mocking of her evil stepsisters, she cared for them without bitterness or malice. Nonetheless, the weary girl felt abandoned, alone, and unloved. When *we* resent someone, even someone who abuses us, we leave open unseen spiritual doors that will attract hidden bitterness unless we release it.

Drifting back to the familiar tale, there appears a "fairy godmother" who saw Cinderella's wounded state and offered her the chance to attend the ball.

The fairy godmother said to Cinderella, "Well, you have what you need to go to the ball; are you not pleased with it?"

"Oh, yes," she cried; "but must I go in these nasty rags?"

The godmother then touched her, and her clothes instantly turned into cloth of gold and silver, beset with jewels. This done, she gave her a pair of glass slippers, the prettiest in the whole world. Being thus decked out, she climbed up into her coach, which she had formed from a pumpkin; but her godmother, above all things, commanded her not to stay past midnight, telling her that if she stayed one moment longer, the coach would be changed back into a pumpkin, her horses into mice, her coachman a rat, her footmen lizards, and her clothes rags as before.

She promised she would leave the ball before midnight, and then drove away, scarcely able to contain her joy. The king's son was told that a great princess, whom nobody knew, had arrived, so he ran out to receive her. He gave her his hand as she alighted from the coach, and led her into the hall, among all the company. There was immediately a profound silence. Everyone stopped dancing, and the violins ceased to play, so entranced was everyone with the singular beauties of the unknown newcomer.

Nothing was then heard but a confused noise of, "How beautiful she is! How beautiful she is!"

All it took was one touch from the godmother (a person who protects and nurtures), and Cinderella was seen to be a beautiful, adorned princess. Like Cinderella, in our pain we wept and cried out. Our grief may have been the result of loss, rejection, abuse, loneliness, or even secret sin. The Holy Spirit, our nurturing Protector, gave us revelation of a great Prince and His kingdom. In joy we received the truth into our heart and instantly felt new—complete and beautiful. Our filthy rags were replaced with royal garments.

I delight greatly in the LORD;
my soul rejoices in my God.
For he has clothed me with garments of salvation
and arrayed me in a robe of righteousness,
as a bridegroom adorns his head like a priest,
and as a bride adorns herself with her jewels. (Isaiah 61:10 NIV)

Even as the prince waited with expectancy for the princess nobody knew, Jesus was waiting for you! Father God and His Son see you untainted by sin, rejection, or pain—you're lovely. Since before the foundations of the world God has waited expectantly for the day of your arrival and your spiritual marriage to His Son.

The king himself, old as he was, could not help watching her, and telling the queen softly that it was a long time since he had seen so beautiful and lovely a creature as Cinderella.

The king's son led her to the most honorable seat, and afterward invited her to dance with him. She danced so very gracefully that they admired her all the more. A fine meal was served, but the young prince ate not a morsel, so intently was he busied in gazing on her. The king's son was always by her, and never ceased his compliments and kind speeches to her. All this was so far from being tiresome to her, and, indeed, she quite forgot what her godmother had told her. She thought that it was no later than eleven when she counted the clock striking twelve. She jumped up and fled, as nimble as a deer. The prince followed, but he could not overtake her. She left behind one of her glass slippers, which the prince picked up most carefully. She reached home, but quite out of breath, and in her nasty old clothes, having nothing left of all her finery but one of the little slippers, the mate to the one she had dropped.

When the two sisters returned from the ball, Cinderella asked them if they had been well entertained. They told her yes, but that a beautiful princess had hurried away immediately when it struck twelve, and with so much haste that she dropped one of her little glass slippers, the prettiest in the world, which the king's son had picked up; that he had done nothing but look at her all the time at the ball, and that most certainly he was very much in love with the beautiful person who owned the glass slipper.

What they said was very true; a few days later, the king's son proclaimed that he would marry her whose foot this slipper would fit. They began to try it on the princesses, then the duchesses and all the court, but in vain; it was brought to the two sisters, who did all they possibly could to force their feet into the slipper, but they did not succeed.

Cinderella, who saw all this, and knew that it was her slipper, said to them, laughing, "Let me see if it will not fit me."

Her sisters burst out laughing, and began to banter with her. The gentleman who was sent to try the slipper looked earnestly at

Cinderella, and, finding her very beautiful, said that it was only fair that she should try as well, and that he had orders to let everyone try.

The king's noble granted Cinderella favor . . . and all the while the sisters were mocking. Has this happened to you? You prayed for favor, looked for a breakthrough from the bondage of the past, longed for your prince charming. Devils laughed; evil men taunted. Others reminded you of your lack of worth. The cycle of torment seems endless. But look what happens to Cinderella.

The lord had her sit down, and, putting the slipper to her foot, he found that it went on very easily, fitting her as if it had been made of wax. Her two sisters were greatly astonished, but then even more so, when Cinderella pulled out of her pocket the other slipper, and put it on her other foot. Then in came her godmother and touched Cinderella's clothes, making them richer and more magnificent than any of those she had worn before.

And now her two sisters found her to be that fine, beautiful lady whom they had seen at the ball. They threw themselves at her feet to beg pardon for all the ill treatment they had made her undergo. Cinderella took them up, and, as she embraced them, said that she forgave them with all her heart, and wanted them always to love her.

She was taken to the young prince, dressed as she was. He thought she was more charming than before, and, a few days after, married her. Cinderella, who was no less good than beautiful, gave her two sisters lodgings in the palace, and that very same day matched them with two great lords of the court.[1]

The shoe fit Cinderella! The other shoe verified to those present that she was indeed the ball's guest of honor. No longer a victim, she now represented the prestige of a princess; her disgrace and dishonor immediately were vanquished, and the eyes of her deceived sisters were opened. Wounded Cinderella could have never forgiven and blessed her abusers, but victorious Cinderella lifted up from the floor her wicked sisters, embraced them, forgave them, and blessed them!

Her prince thought she was perfect, and he bestowed upon her all the pageantry of a royal. He never inquired as to her past; he wasn't worried about any rags she'd once worn. He didn't even inquire as to why she'd fled on the night of the ball—he accepted her for who she was. Rags and all, Cinderella was his heart's desire.

MORAL OF THE STORY

He raises the poor from the dust
and lifts the needy from the ash heap;
he seats them with princes,
with the princes of their people. (Psalm 113:7–8 NIV)

God gives us beauty to replace the ashes of our lives. Cinderella once slept at the fireplace hearth, her clothes and skin soiled with cinder; she had known the fire of suffering. But she chose to love her accusers, to minister to them with grace . . . and the king's men offered her a new beginning. When a person is spiritually healed, she becomes a rare treasure, revealing the essence of God's love. Grace is priceless— mercy flows freely. Grace under pressure is more beautiful than a new hairdo, a new set of clothes, or a fancy title. It's a true gift of life. Without it, nothing is possible; with it, one can do anything.

Cinderella's godmother gave her grace to behave like a queen. Our Father God also teaches us that from our broken heart we can forgive and walk forward in queenly holiness. No doubt it's of great advantage to have intelligence, courage, talent, and common sense, for *every* good and perfect gift comes from heaven. However, even these will never bring you peace and fulfillment without the blessing of a genuine intimate relationship with Jesus, your heavenly Prince.

MY PRINCE

Soon after I became a Christian at fifteen, our youth pastor taught us to pray for our future spouses. Immediately taking this to heart, I began to pray for God to bless, protect, and prepare the man I'd one day marry.

One Sunday night in 1969 I sang a solo at First Baptist Church, Houston. After the service, evangelist Dr. Ted Roe and his wife came to me and asked, "Do you know Eddie Smith?" When I said that I didn't, these kind strangers tried to convince me that Eddie was my future husband.

Amazingly, the following year I met Eddie at a downtown Christian coffeehouse, and within weeks we were serious about our relationship. So I prayed for God's revelation about the future. Immediately, the Spirit reminded me of my earlier conversation with the Roes. Other confirmations I sought were my parents' approval, what my friends thought of us as a couple, and what my pastor, Dr. John Bisagno, felt about Eddie. (He knew Eddie well—they'd worked in evangelism together.) Then I asked the Spirit for revelation from God's Word. Prophetic words from Scripture and a witness in my heart convinced me that Eddie was my soul mate.

Because of Eddie's busy traveling schedule, and because of our youthful impatience, we decided to forego a formal church wedding. I was nonetheless disappointed, as it had been my lifelong dream to have a beautiful wedding dress and walk the church aisle toward my prince. I'd even seen a wedding dress in my mind's eye while in prayer.

When Ted learned that Eddie and I wanted to be married, we met him at his downtown office. On July 14, 1970, in blue jeans and tennis shoes, we were wed, with Ted officiating. Right after our vows, we drove to Eddie's next crusade in Gulfport, Mississippi.

All marriages present challenges, and we've certainly had ours as well. We've cried, struggled, laughed, prayed, dreamed, argued, played, loved, and shared in abundance and in loss. But through it all, Eddie and I have had a lifetime love affair.

We in Christian ministry often have a signature message that defines our calling. Mine is about an intimate relationship with Jesus—the spiritual bride and groom. Yet one desire remained in my heart all these years . . . my longest-held and most treasured prayer request was yet to be fulfilled. This was a secret between the Lord Jesus and me.

THE BRIDE

My miracle has come! My oldest prayer request has been answered! Eddie and I got married! Well, not exactly . . . we'd *been* married. But we recently celebrated our thirty-fifth anniversary, and this was unlike any previous celebration.

My older sister, Jo Ann, asked me to join her at a bridal shop to help select a dress for a fancy office ball. On the phone I tried to convince her that the bridal shop wasn't the best place to find the dress she was looking for, yet she insisted that her friend promised "they had just the right dress for her."

As I entered BridesMart, there were dozens of mannequins displaying beautiful wedding dresses. Before I could catch myself, I reflectively mused, "Oh, I want a wedding dress." Jo Ann approached and handed me a rolled-up piece of paper tied with a bow.

"What's this?" I asked.

"Read it!" she said with nervous excitement in her voice.

I untied and read the small scroll. *You are here to select your wedding dress for a July wedding ceremony to be funded by family and friends!*

What?! I was shocked! I was thrilled! I was crying . . . and I was confused.

Eddie walked from behind the mirrored wall with a rose and a card in his hand. As he approached me, it was as if I'd never before laid eyes on him—and my heart leapt as it had when I saw him for the first time. I fell in love with Eddie all over again! Suddenly a group of my close friends emerged from behind the clothing racks where they'd been hidden. They were there to surprise me also.

"Alice, will you marry me again?" Eddie sweetly asked. I fell into his arms as I answered, "Yes, I will marry you again. I love you with all my heart." In BridesMart that day I chose a gorgeous white wedding dress with a long beautiful train. It was everything I'd ever prayed for and dreamed of.

The church was adorned with wispy white flowers draped on the pews, on the floor, into the aisles, and up onto the stage. Tall, white columns laced with flowers stood majestically on the platform. The fresh scent of arrangements filled the air as if we were standing at the altar of incense near the Holy of Holies. Our four handsome children were the groomsmen and bridesmaids, joining us at the altar to confirm our union. Our girls each wore purple dresses, the symbol of royalty. Our grandchildren were perfect as junior groomsmen and flower girls. The cakes were sculpted as for a king and queen, and twin ice swans glistened in the light of the reception hall.

Like icing on the cake, Ted Roe, now a businessman in Phoenix, flew to Houston and skillfully performed the ceremony, speaking eloquently of how one day we will forever be with our heavenly bridegroom. Warmth of friends and family made everything extra-special. This celebration was a testament to the prophetic promise that God never forgets the desires of His bride.

Dreams do come true. As Christ's spiritual bride, my entire life has been enthusiastically devoted to Him and to prayer. I prayed for thirty-five years to have a church wedding with a beautiful white dress, and to walk an aisle in covenant love as a tangible expression of a spiritual truth. Jesus delighted to answer the longstanding request of which only He and I knew.

Jesus is your Prince Charming, too. He has washed you whiter than snow, and He has clothed you in a white wedding gown of righteousness. He rejoices to call you His own. Are you willing to walk the aisle toward Him?

One last look back at Cinderella, to make sure we don't miss the best part: The king called for "a royal ball to which all maidens of noble birth" were to respond. Her father was a widower, *"of the king's* court." Do you see it? *Cinderella had actually been royalty all along!* That she hadn't felt like royalty didn't change the truth about her. She *was* royalty!

Cinderella had lived as a victim when all the benefits of the kingdom were already hers. The day came, however, when she stepped out of her painful past and into her future destiny. All it took was one glimpse of the prince. Have you caught a glimpse of your heavenly Prince? Once you do, you will never be the same.

Your Prince Charming has come to rescue you from the ashes. No need to cower in the shadows of your yesterdays. Put on the glass slippers and walk confidently on a new path beyond the lies of your past. I now pronounce you, "Healed in Christ Jesus!"

Testimonies

FREEDOM FROM BONDAGE

Feeling vulnerable is normal in certain situations. However, what you do with these feelings will shape your character and your future. Some people fall in love with the victim spirit. They caress their wounds, dwell on their feelings, harbor unforgiveness, and use it all to gather attention from friends and family. I knew the torment of this spirit, and I've had to shut the door on it for myself.

What's tragic about this devilish spirit is not only the way it's acquired but also the destruction it can cause in our lives. In the midst of the dry and difficult times everyone experiences, it's easy for us to feel hopeless or lonely, and the enemy picks up on our weakness and sends his demons to seduce us. In these tough seasons when we should call on our heavenly Father, many of us tend to rely instead on feedback from friends or seek comfort in drugs, alcohol, cigarettes, or antidepressants.

We think, "Why me? No matter what I do, I'm wrong. I'm a failure, and I'm unloved." Even children can have these thoughts, and when the devil finds them confused and vulnerable, he's found the perfect opportunity to victimize.

I was blessed to be born into a Christian family. Sunday morning, Sunday night, and Wednesday night we were in the church my parents had planted. My dad had been the associate pastor, and I knew I was special to the members and to my friends—like a pretty little princess.

As a six-year-old, when I heard what Jesus had done for me, my eyes filled with tears as I invited Him into my heart to be my Lord and Savior.

Home life also was secure and good. We had a beautiful brick house in a big suburban city. My older sisters had already married, and my brother, seven years older, attended the local public high school. My mother took me to a private Christian school each morning.

When we faced the economic downturn caused by the 1980s oil-bust in Texas, my parents felt we needed to give up our home. I was confused and angry about having to move. At the age of eight I had no concept of how our budget affected where we lived. I was sad; I didn't want to leave my home or my neighborhood friends.

I will never forget the afternoon we drove over to see our new town-house. The dark skies were gray, the air was windy, and Mom and Dad prayed for our safety as we sat in the car through a tornado alert. Little did I know at the time that soon I would face a dark storm of my own, a storm that would change my life and the lives of my family forever.

I began to feel hopeless and alone in our new area. Not long after, my older brother moved to Dallas to attend a school of ministry. My loneliness festered as I gazed at the empty streets of our neighborhood, wondering, *Does anyone care about me? I'm so bored and lonely. I'd have more friends if I went to regular school and didn't play the stupid piano. Why do I have to be different? Why don't my parents see my problems? What about me?*

I begged my dad to put me into public school, and finally my parents agreed. I enjoyed the teachers and activities, and one day I met a girl named Stacie who happened to live down the street from us. I was excited. I thought all I needed was a friend.

One afternoon when I came home from school, Dad and I sat on the front porch and had a little talk. The sadness in his eyes pierced my soul, because I'd never seen him set aside his charming sense of humor. What he was facing would change the course of our family. He told me we were going to leave our church home. I didn't understand why, especially since it seemed to be the only thing I had left.

This felt like a death in our family—the loss of so many friends and much more. The next weekend, we started looking at other churches.

My isolation grew. One practice in our home was that every Friday night we'd all do something together, but I began to shrug off our family time. I was hurting and angry, and I felt that no one, including my parents, would understand me—I didn't even understand. At this time I started entertaining a victim spirit. I rehearsed how pitiful and unloved I was, and I began to believe lies. The devil had an open door for attack, and boy did he use it.

One day I walked over to Stacie's, thinking she was my only hope for a good time. As I entered her house, the sound of girls laughing loudly lifted my heart. Ambling through her back gate, I saw her and two other girls circled around a tank of gasoline, and I watched as they inhaled fumes and laughed hysterically. The gas can came my way, and they announced it was my turn. I took four deep breaths and huffed my way into oblivion. Immediately I was cured—no pain, no stress, no sadness. I was left without a care in the world.

From the gasoline fumes I turned to potpourri to get a high; from potpourri I went to spray paint for new thrills. Every now and then we'd steal liquor from Stacie's mom's stash and get drunk. It didn't take long before I had two more neighborhood friends—the wrong kind, but friends. The enemy's camp was set up to keep me a victim and to shape my destiny for failure.

Soon the inhalants turned into a wide span of street drugs: marijuana, cocaine, crack, LSD, speed, PCP, ice, ecstasy, and 'shrooms became my comforters. Addiction controlled my thoughts and actions. By fifteen I'd been arrested twice and kicked out of three schools. Once a straight-A student, a cheerleader with high ranks and Texas beauty titles, now I was a crackhead with a horrible attitude. I knew I had a problem, but I didn't care. My parents were deeply grieved and unable to control me. The conviction I once felt for my wrong behavior had finally left, and I'd numbed my emotions. I told God to leave me alone, and I ignored my family's guidance.

There was little hope for finishing high school. I couldn't even remain in my last junior high for one semester because of my rebellion. I heard about a Christian school twenty minutes away, where class was only two days a week. When the administration looked over my conduct record and shook their heads, we begged them for a chance to make things right; I had one month to catch up to a freshman academic level, and it wasn't easy but I did it. With the intensive outpatient treatment the courts demanded as part of my probation, studies seemed impossible, but I made it.

My close friends started dying. One died in a drunken accident, one in a drug overdose; one was murdered, another shot himself. One just dropped dead on her kitchen floor—her family still doesn't know how she died. I was beaten by a group of men while protecting a girl friend who'd passed out. I had my tires slashed; I crashed my car while intoxicated; I was raped; I was sexually assaulted by two girl friends. I learned that the world of drugs and life on the street was cutthroat: You either hold your own or you won't survive. The devil is a ruthless slavemaster. You serve him, or he'll kill you.

Though Mom and Dad were deeply confused by my behavior, they wouldn't give up on me. At times I could sense their intercession and spiritual warfare, but I ignored the warnings. I began to pocket change from selling dope, and on weekdays I worked for extra drug money. I saved enough money to move out on my own so I could "use" anytime I wanted.

God knew my perverted plan and threw in an extra surprise. Reckless and without a moral conscience, I was seventeen when I got pregnant. I'd always wanted to be a mother, thinking that having someone to care for would fill my empty heart. My child *is* a blessing, but being pregnant did not stop my drug use. I was engaged to be married to the young man I loved, but two weeks before my wedding I got a call from my fiancé: strung out on cocaine, he said he wasn't interested in starting a family. He moved across town, leaving me with a devastated and abandoned heart. The victim mindset and cycle were fully entrenched in my soul. Life was a constant roller coaster of emotions.

Addiction was my first priority, a fact I was having a hard time hiding. I decided to leave the job I'd held for five years. I made a game of deceiving my colleagues and my family so they wouldn't know my income was from selling drugs full time. The devil doesn't pay very well; all my bills were due, I didn't have any money, and I was drowning in the mess of my life.

The rude awakening happened one winter afternoon. I was sleeping late when the police broke through my apartment door, raided my home, and took me to jail. I served two and a half months in the county jail, and, ironically, it was there that the God I was running from came to comfort and love me. When I bottomed out, Jesus Christ became my best friend.

All the users on the outside of the jail bars who claimed to be my friends were nowhere to be found when I needed help. With the huge mess I faced, I was at the mercy of a judge who planned to put me in the state penitentiary for four years. My faith was unwavering as I trusted the Lord, seeking His forgiveness and strength and earnestly praying I wouldn't miss the next four years of my son's life. God heard and answered my prayers.

That is the story of my past. Gone, forever behind me. Today I'm happy I've made the choice not to let my past determine who I will become. Today I am free from being the victim. I slammed the door. I pray for those who hurt me, and I accept the things that I cannot change.

Life is what you make it. I've learned to handle my tough times rather than letting them handle me. With the Lord in my heart leading me through His Spirit, I know I'll overcome. If you've read this story and know someone suffering from drug addiction, reach out; show God's unconditional love in a practical way. The seeds of love and prayers you plant in a life will one day produce a rich harvest. I know, because I am one!

FROM TORMENT TO TESTAMENT

I'm an African-American man who grew up in a decent neighborhood. I never knew my real father, a fact which I believe was my open door to bitterness. Mom said he left the house one day to go buy some things and never came back.

My grandmother was religious, and I would constantly ask her questions, but she could never satisfy my inner hunger for God. With Mom it was different—we rarely went to church, probably because we moved all the time. My grandmother kept us, and we were often bused to Sunday school at a mostly white Baptist congregation. I remember they talked so much about Jesus, I used to say, "I don't want to hear about Jesus, I want to hear about God." I was about eight at the time.

After my mom remarried there were twelve of us. Domestic violence and abuse kept us constantly afraid, and even at a young age I found myself praying for help and safety—I'd heard in church how Jesus said something about getting into your closet to pray. I realized the power of prayer and experienced great results. Not long after I saw *The Ten Commandments* (with Charlton Heston) and noticed how Moses talked to a burning bush, I saw that same bush (so I thought!) about three miles from our house. I ran to it to pray, following Moses' example. It was late when I got back home.

I felt others' pain as if the hurts were mine. None of my brothers or sisters was very obedient to my mother, but I obeyed. During my childhood I went through abuse—mental, physical, and sexual. I think my whole life was plagued by demons before now, but most American Christians are afraid to talk about demons, often not even realizing that they're real.

I liked school and was doing okay, though I never was super smart. Work was enjoyable; my first job was as a dishwasher/busboy. I loved it. In ninth grade I was in art class drawing a portrait for a contest when my teacher, Mr. Frances, invited me to a wiener roast. That Friday, after we ate, we listened to a salvation message. My teacher came up to me and told me all about Jesus, and I got saved that night. Over a period of time he would pick me up for church.

One Sunday Mr. Frances brought me home after church and everyone was still sleeping. I turned the TV on to watch a service. When they showed a close-up of an open Bible, my eyes began to feel funny; next thing I know, Jesus' face was as if it was etched in the Bible's very words. The vision was so real and startling that I immediately turned off the TV, only to still see a shadowy face of Jesus. I ran to the back room, laid on the bed, and shut my eyes real tight. When I reopened them, the face of Jesus was still there. I closed my eyes again and fell asleep. Years would pass before I'd understand that vision.

No one else in my home was saved, and the experience I'd had at fifteen quickly fell away. Tragically, I was coached by a friend to burglarize houses, and I gave in. One night we robbed five in the neighborhood. I began to think I was an expert, so I started on my own rampage against humanity. I also began to drink and stay out all night. (When I was younger my cousin had introduced me to marijuana. I remember feeling on one occasion when I smoked that my soul had been opened to a dark force.)

My mom would be furious with me, but there was nothing she could do. I was out of control and had surrendered to a sinister influence. I was an early victim, and now I victimized others. My siblings saw how I was, and they'd warn that I was headed for prison. I'd pay no attention.

Demonic spirits drove my life. I could feel them stalking and harassing me. One night I came home drunk from a party and sat around until late, then I broke into a house where six or seven guys were sleeping. Nervous but driven by Satan and alcohol, I opened the icebox, found a beer, and drank it fast. Then I took a few hundred dollars out of the wallets in their pants and left.

Another time, at 5:00 A.M., out of money, bored, and demonized, I saw a lady clerk inside a convenience store. Under the influence of drugs and alcohol, I didn't shut out the tormenting evil forces. I went inside and pretended to look at magazines until the clerk finished with customers.

A great battle was raging in my mind—part of me didn't want to do this. But I did. When the store was empty, I walked to the end of the counter and asked for matches. When she came toward me, I grabbed her and pulled out my knife. She said the money was down at the other end.

Just then a truck pulled up, so I pushed her to the back of the store. I was so scared and my adrenalin was flowing like crazy. Standing in front of her, I felt the very presence of evil. I was in trouble for pulling a knife, and the voices in my head were saying, *Stab her, stab her, she's going to tell—stab her.*

Suddenly she grabbed the sharp blade with her hand, and it cut her as I pulled it away. I went blank, and after I came to I had stabbed this innocent woman four times. I can't get out of my head that as I looked into her eyes I literally saw her dying. Her blue eyes began to fade as the light of life was leaving her body. She died in my presence.

Afterward I felt emptiness, as though part of me had died also. It would be years before I could see Jesus cleansing my life by His precious blood. Now I realize that John 10:10 is real—Jesus said He came to give life, life more abundant, but the thief has come to steal, kill, and destroy. That night I knew what that thief is capable of doing through a wounded human being. I was that person.

In 1979 I was captured and sentenced to twenty years. I was stationed in a prison unit, where hard work was instilled, though even with that I couldn't sleep.

I became friends with two other guys. One gave his heart to Jesus, and from that time on he would bug us to do the same. One week the prison was having a three-day revival, so I went with my friend. On the last night at the altar call my friends were nagging me to go forward. I thought I'd go up and pray a little and say I accepted Jesus. However, when I bent down to the altar I collapsed into a loud cry for God to help me. I joined a prayer group in the prison called Prayer Fellowship.

Starting around 1982, God had begun to move on me in prayer. Funny, though, that most people I knew had no idea about prayer or intercession. I remember finding a book on prayer, and in it the author said Jesus prayed for an hour so He expected his disciples to pray for an hour. At that time I couldn't pray for an hour, but as I submitted to pray more, my experiences were heightened by the Holy Spirit. God's presence was so strong I had to stop praying at times. He was training me with hands-on experience of travailing prayer. I didn't know anything about the disciplines of the Christian life and couldn't find anyone to mentor me.

In April 1986 I was released early. The first two months were great . . . then Satan reared his ugly head. I didn't know at the time, but all the gates of trauma, bitterness, and anger were still open in my life. Strongholds had been established in me, and I didn't know how to stop the cycle. Through my complacency and my failure to get involved in a good church, I became cold and distant to Jesus. I was discouraged and weary.

I connected with my cousin, who reintroduced me to cigarettes and marijuana. I forgot about Jesus. I was exposed, living like I never knew Him. Back into burglary and stealing, I ventured further and further from the Lord, even though He put believers right in my path.

I met a young woman and immediately moved in with her. One evening, when we were about to go to sleep, God spoke to me in a clear voice in the quietness: *You need to repent.* It startled me, and as I thought about the message I knew it was the Lord. I got up and began to read through my Bible. I read in Hebrews 4:7 about hearing His voice and not hardening your heart.

For a week I thought on these words, only to have my heart harden. I went back to living it up with my girlfriend. It was like I opened a door wider than ever before and bees swarmed in to sting me. The enemy took advantage of my ongoing rebellion.

Anger had been part of my life since I was little. One Monday night I was watching the NFL on TV, and during the break I looked in on my sleeping girlfriend. At that moment an eerie sensation came over me and in my head a voice said, *Stab her,* but I shook it off and went back into the living room. After the game I listened to music that generated thoughts of revenge and violence. Filled with liquor, I got into my car and drove to the place where I'd been fired. For no reason at all, I stabbed two females that worked there. Two days later I was arrested and received two concurrent forty-five-year sentences.

I was cold toward the Lord and didn't want anything to do with Him. One day I was alone in my cell, lying on my bunk, not thinking of anything. God spoke softly to my heart: *Look at you, you're right back to where you started. Rededicate yourself to me.* I got up this time and cried out to Him in deep, gut-level repentance.

I'd never before felt the peace and freedom that came into my heart that day. From then on, God started ministering to me and teaching me all over again. The Spirit began to lead me back to a prayer ministry. I received a book by Leonard Ravenhill, powerfully emphasizing prayer. I learned about travailing prayer. My relationship with God became more intimate.

Supernatural visitations with the Holy Spirit opened my heart to see the demonic spirits that had gripped me. I began to experience deliverance from them. The more and more I sought the Word of God and believed it, the more freedom I received. Jesus set me free from a demonic web that cost me everything, although the end result is that I've found everything in Christ Jesus.

Like Alice Smith says, "You only have time in your life for one passion, so choose your passion carefully." I have chosen my passion and it's Jesus Christ. There's a hidden world out there, unseen but real and more powerful than the one we see. I know the reality of bondage and evil and rebellion. Now I know the joy of freedom and victory.

Parents who have kids—pray and pray and pray for them. Tell them early how to become a believer and show them by living the

Christian life. My life was ruined, but God had mercy on me despite the lives I took and the people I hurt. Because of Jesus I know His forgiveness, healing, and delivering power.

This I know for sure: Somebody prayed me through. I likewise have prayed many people through, breaking Satan's grip. It has been miracle after miracle. Intercession is my calling, but Jesus is my passion. Don't stay a victim—be a victor today!

VICTIM NO MORE

All I could do was sit and stare out my window at the house across the street.

Don't tell or else kept running through my mind. I wanted my mommy, but I couldn't tell. Fear utterly gripped me as I started to cry.

"What am I going to do?" I asked myself. Even though I was only nine, I was sure I was pregnant. One thing for sure, I promised myself: I would never be alone in my violator's house again. My problem was that his little sister, Pat, was my best friend. So I made up stories, excuses, and reasons why I couldn't go to see her if I knew her brother was home.

Pat and I did all the things nine-year-old girls do. We played dress-up and other games. We talked about boys and laughed a lot. We were at her house the day my life changed forever. Her brother, Ted (not his real name), asked if he could talk to me. He was a tall teen, known as a prankster among family and friends. I was shocked and frightened when Ted showed me some baby birds he had skewered through the neck. His sinister laugh still rings in my mind.

When I broke into tears, sitting out of plain sight of Ted, he moved in "to console me." I calmed down, but before I had realized what happened, he moved closer and pinned my body against the outside wall of the basement. "Shhh . . . it's okay, I just need to know something." Ted kept repeating, "Shhh . . . don't cry, it's all right."

I was stunned and limp. Afterward, he sternly warned me not to tell what he had done or else someone would get hurt. Remembering what he'd done to those baby birds, I believed him.

During the fourth grade I had to change schools. At my new one, after a class celebration ended after dark, I said good-bye to my friends and started my walk home. On my way I realized a boy was following me. At first I didn't think anything about it; he was on a bike, which wasn't so unusual. I began to be alarmed, though, when he made several circles to ride by again. Then he spoke to me with such vile words that my heart nearly jumped into my throat. I picked up my pace as he threatened to rape me in a nearby field, and I could hear in my mind my father's instruction: "If you're ever in trouble, don't make eye contact. Keep walking; don't give the person the satisfaction of thinking they've got you." My weak legs regained strength, and I kept my eyes locked in the direction of my home, assured that once I got there I'd be safe.

My father, wanting justice, used me as bait to catch this boy. Once again I was in between my violator and my safe haven. It seemed a door had been opened, and now I was fending off unwanted advances. Somehow the word *no* had no meaning to those who saw me as an easy mark. I felt naked and unprotected even by those who were responsible for my safety. I became angry and decided I would be my own protector . . . but my anger turned on me and I became its prisoner. Like an unruly monster, rage and fear took control and left me with deep sorrows.

I was looking for love and acceptance when someone told me about Jesus Christ. At the time my greatest desire was to be free from torment. Like a whirlwind romance, I accepted Jesus, was water-baptized, and received the baptism of the Holy Spirit within only three weeks. My faithful Lord began working in me through dreams and revelations about my tormentor. I realized I didn't have to stay the way I was. The father of lies had deceived me, and now my eyes were opening. I found that I was striving for perfection, driven by a need for approval. I longed to be validated, desired to be heard, and was fearful of disappointing

God. Most painful of all was when I realized I was angry with Him.

Mine has been a journey of discovery and revelation. I became aware of the methods I'd used that kept me in bondage. I had hidden myself with layers of body fat, drove myself to exhaustion being the perfect mom and housewife, and harshly scourged myself for any failures. I was judgmental, impatient, and unkind. God had mercy on me and brought His agents of truth along my path. Through deliverance, training, accountability, self-examination, confession, repentance, and renouncing, the tormentors no longer had control, and I was experiencing true freedom in Christ.

I am the mother of seven children and grandmother to seven. The freedom I see in my children gives me such joy and gratitude, knowing that had it not been for the Lord, they wouldn't be the people they are today. By His grace I've moved from needing approval to giving approval; from fear to knowing His great love and divine patience. I've had the privilege of traveling around the world to see firsthand how the name of Jesus sets captives free. I've walked foreign soil and partnered with nationals to break the bonds of the enemy and impart the dominion of God. I've cried, laughed, and prayed with many Christians and have received a deposit of the Father's heart for His children. I'm most blessed and grateful that He who has begun a good work in me is faithful to complete it. I'm in His hands. He has set me free, and He can set you free as well.

A PRAYER LEADER'S JOURNEY

I have only one memory of seeing my parents together. They divorced when I was in preschool, and my mother remarried about the time I started kindergarten. I had two siblings: my sister, two years older, and my fraternal twin brother. Our stepfather, a mechanic, worked on cars in our yard. I was afraid of him because he drank heavily and would slap me when intoxicated. He'd often yell for one of us to bring him a particular tool, and we'd run to the toolbox to find it. As a five-year-old boy I didn't have a clue what he wanted, but I knew he'd hit me if he had to come for it himself.

When I was six or seven we moved to the small central Arkansas town where my grandfather lived. Things worsened from there. I didn't realize that physical and mental abuse aren't normal; I just assumed I was a bad boy who deserved what I got. The abuse was meant to humiliate and shame us, and those early traumas opened the door to problems later in life.

One Saturday my stepfather made my brother and I wear our sister's dresses and took us to town. We were forced to walk up and down the street while the farmers laughed at us. The dress was all I was wearing, and I can still hear my grandfather's laughter as he would lift my dress and expose my nakedness. I don't even remember what we did to be punished.

My first exposure to homosexuality came one evening when two older boys invited my brother and me to go for a car ride with them. They gave my brother candy, and I watched as they then took turns sodomizing him. For some reason I thought this was okay. When I was about eight, it started happening to me.

Once when my mother was out of the house my stepfather took me by the arm and led me into the bedroom. He told me to take my pants down and lay across the bed. I thought I was going to get a spanking but didn't know what for. As he violated me I cried out. He slapped me and said "shut up—that doesn't hurt." From then on I tried to remain quiet.

Other times he demanded that I sexually satisfy him. All the while he assured me this was normal. I'm sure my mother never knew anything about it, but there was a time when I began to understand that it wasn't right.

I was about twelve when we moved to Huntsville, Alabama. My sister was living with one of our uncles and my brother lived with our grandfather. By this time we had three younger half-sisters. Out of curiosity, one of my half-sisters and I began to experiment sexually when no one was home. All I knew about sex was what I had learned from my stepfather.

One day as we were eating lunch, my half-sister blurted out that she had touched my private parts. I knew it was wrong to do these things so I blurted back, "You did not!" Well, I knew I was in trouble—in fact, I was sure my stepfather would *kill* me when he came home. However, that evening, instead of receiving the beating of my life, he sexually assaulted me. Things were unbearable in those days. I ran away a lot but would always be brought back.

Finally I asked to be placed in a boys' home in Kansas. This home held about a hundred of us, ages six through eighteen, in five or six large houses. It was also a farm—our work duties included vegetables, beef, and dairy cattle. They had a school too, and when we had a spelling or a math test we received a swat with a paddle for every wrong answer. With that motivation, you might think I'd have learned how to spell, but I didn't.

By the time I went to the home I was old enough to be sexually active. There were basically three types of boys there: young boys not sexually active, older boys who were, and homosexual boys. The homosexual boys delighted in making themselves available to the older boys. Also, one of the custodians was homosexual. I had several encounters with him.

My father eventually married four times. I only knew two of his wives besides my mother. I was fifteen when he came and took me from the boys' home. He was living in Topeka, Kansas, and it was there I began to encounter girls. Strangely, I seemed to always attract the promiscuous ones and soon had several encounters. Now I understand how the open door of victimization was like a neon light to spiritual darkness.

Something happened in Topeka that caused me to hate my father. It was summer, and school was out, but my father always woke me when he went to work, expecting me to get out of bed. I would smart off and tell him to go to hell, but he'd persist until I got up.

On one occasion I was in the bathroom with the door locked. I don't remember what I'd said, but my father broke down the door, ripped off my underwear, and pushed me out into the kitchen in front of my stepmother. Then he left for work. I was furious, and she was embarrassed. Strangely, I hated my father more for that humiliation than for all my stepfather had ever done. There was a picture of my father on the wall, so I took a knife and stabbed it repeatedly.

That day I left and went to Pueblo, Colorado, to stay with some of my stepmother's relatives. My stepmother had two children, a boy two years older and a girl my age. Nancy Jo was beautiful, and I fell madly in love with her. She was the first girl I ever respected—I would have walked on red-hot coals for her. I wouldn't allow myself to even think about doing anything disrespectful with her. She was my first love.

Later that year my father and stepmother moved from Topeka to Denver. My stepbrother, Nancy Jo, and I moved in with them. My stepbrother was into guns, and from time to time we'd go out to the country and shoot targets. On one occasion, I took four of the bullets, stuck them in my pocket, and later showed them to Nancy Jo, telling her I was going to kill my father. She told him, and he had me arrested. I was in jail for a couple days, and when I returned home, my stepbrother and Nancy Jo were back in Pueblo along with the guns.

GOD AT WORK

About this time God began to work in my life. In Denver our family was invited to attend a church. At the end of one service, someone approached me and asked if I wanted to get saved. I wasn't sure what he meant, but I said yes and went forward.

On the way home my father made fun of me and called me a "holy roller." (He was a Freemason, and in Topeka he'd dabbled in the occult.) He did this for several days and I never went back to that church, nor did the church ever contact me.

Something changed in my life at sixteen. Although I hated my father, I no longer wanted to kill him. I still showed him a lot of disrespect. I made fun of him and destroyed things that belonged to him.

One time when I was eighteen I got into a fistfight with him. As an electrician, my dad followed construction, so we moved a lot. From my high school years I didn't spend a full year in one place. I finally graduated in Charlestown, Indiana. My father was moving on to another job, so I went back to Denver. When I couldn't find a job there, I joined the Navy.

After basic training I was stationed in Memphis for further training in aircraft maintenance. Late one evening I was on the streets and noticed a group of people leaving a large auditorium; they'd attended a Gospel Quartet concert. Suddenly a car caught fire, and some of them stopped to watch the fire department's efforts. Two of these people were an attractive girl and her mother.

I struck up a conversation with them, and the next thing I knew we were in a cab on the way to their home. My mind was fully focused on this new girl, Jane, and her equally attractive mother. When we arrived, they prepared food and talked with me about the Lord. I continued to see Jane for the next couple weeks as she loyally shared her faith with me.

One evening at the base, the Spirit convicted me to give my life to Christ, and I prayed to receive Jesus as my Savior. At the time I was a smoker; I told the Lord that I couldn't serve Him and smoke. I asked Him to take away the desire. Remarkably, I flushed my remaining pack down the toilet, and I never smoked again.

When I got off duty, I went to Jane's home and told her what had happened. At first they didn't believe me. But in subsequent weeks, especially when I was filled with the Holy Spirit, they were convinced. Life with the Lord was wonderful in those early days. I was growing in Him and felt a call on my life.

Later that summer Jane and her mother moved to Mississippi, and

I was left without a friend. Sadly, I began hanging out with promiscuous girls again, but it was from within the church this time. A father of one church girl I impregnated, arranged for her to have an abortion, and this was before abortions were legal. Not long after I was transferred to Newfoundland and spent the remainder of my Navy enlistment out of fellowship with Christ.

When I was discharged I enrolled in a Bible School in Dallas. I wanted to serve the Lord, but even there I always seemed to draw promiscuous girls. After two years I married a preacher's daughter and became assistant pastor of his church. He knew my past and kept a tight rein on me. I can say that in the twelve-year marriage I never strayed, but the desire was there. I was miserable in the tragic restlessness of my life, and I eventually left her.

I spent the next four years satisfying my lustful appetite. I don't know how many women I was with or how much damage I caused them and their families. I know I broke up the family of a close friend, caused at least one married woman to have an abortion, and compelled another to have a baby she claimed was mine and not her husband's. Not only did I victimize others, I was a victim of the tormenting devils who drove my life to destruction.

Then I met my second wife, Connie. It started with a lie. I had planned to use her as I had other women and then move on, but she was a godly woman, and the Lord had different plans. As we began to date, God stirred things in my heart that I'd thought were gone forever. Within six months we were married and became involved in our local church.

Sadly, I was still messed up—there were issues I had not worked through and did not share with my wife. About two years into our marriage, a young homeless woman needed a place to stay, and a friend of ours from church allowed her to live with them for a while. Within just a few weeks I reverted to my old ways and became sexually involved with her. Shortly thereafter she moved away, but the damage was done. I stopped serving in our church, and I hoped and prayed my wife would never find out I had betrayed her. However, two years later the woman called my wife and told her all about it. Only God's grace prevented me from losing everything.

AND THEN THE VICTORY CAME

We moved our attendance to another church, and for years I refused to become involved. Connie couldn't understand, but there were two basic reasons. One was the promiscuous pattern I'd struggled with all my life; I didn't feel I was fit to be involved in any kind of ministry. The other was fear—I was terrified that I'd again encounter a situation I couldn't control and would fall into sin. But my loving Father, in all His mercy, had a better plan. I really could identify with Dottie Rambo's song.

He Looked Beyond My Fault and Saw My Need

Amazing Grace, shall always be my song of praise
For it was grace that brought me liberty.
I do not know, just why He came to love me so,
He looked beyond my fault and saw my need.
I shall forever lift mine eyes to Calvary
To view the cross, where Jesus died for me.
How marvelous, His grace that caught my falling soul
He looked beyond my fault and saw my need.[1]

My heavenly Father had a new direction for me: He led me into a lifestyle of prayer and intercession, a path I'd never known and a ministry spent mostly in secret with God. In pursuit of this refreshing personal relationship with Christ, a new calling and anointing developed. Praying for hours a day seemed to be as minutes. I looked to read everything I could find concerning prayer and intercession.

My life was beautiful again, and all went well for about a year. My prayer life was still intact, and my times of intercession were victorious, but there was a problem: Even in times of intense intercession, my mind would suddenly remember some unholy encounter I'd experienced in the past. I tried many ways to get rid of this—I'd stop and rebuke Satan, I'd bind my thoughts; I'd plead the blood over myself—all to no avail. It got to where I was spending more time fighting the enemy in my mind than interceding.

Then one day I asked Alice's husband, Eddie, about it, and he gave me ten steps to personal freedom. With all the sin in my life, it took me two months to work through the steps. Sometimes I'd need to backtrack and do things over again as the Spirit would remind me of things I'd overlooked.

That was four years ago. Today, by God's grace, I am a man of integrity, set free from the sin and victim assignments that had me bound most of my life. I have forgiven my abusers and set the record straight on those who have hurt me. I am no longer attracted to promiscuous women, nor do I attract them. Today I often work with men, many who are bound as I was for so long. When I meet such a man, I give him Eddie Smith's book, *Breaking the Enemy's Grip*.[2]

And I want you to know: You *can* achieve victory in your life. Free at last! Free at last! Thank God Almighty, I am free at last!

> The law of the Spirit of life in Christ Jesus hath made me free from the law of sin and death. (Romans 8:2)

Suggested Reading

Anderson, Neil. *Victory Over the Darkness*. Ventura, CA: Regal, 2000.

Bean, Leroy. *The Garden Within*. Newark, NJ: End Time Wave Publishing, 2003.

Bevere, John. *The Devil's Door*. Lake Mary, FL: Charisma House, 1996.

Bonner, Mickey. *Brokenness, the Forgotten Factor*. Houston, TX: Mickey Bonner Evangelistic Association, 1996.

Bosworth, F. F. *Christ the Healer*. Grand Rapids, MI: Fleming H. Revell, 1973.

Burk, Arthur. *Relentless Generational Blessings*. Whittier, CA: Plumbline Ministries, 2003.

————. *Overcoming the Victim Spirit*. Whittier, CA: Plumbline Ministries, 2001.

Christenson, Larry. *The Renewed Mind*. Minneapolis, MN: Bethany House, 1974.

Coates, Jan. *Set Free*. Minneapolis, MN: Bethany House, 2005.

Daniels, Kimberly. *Clean House, Strong House*. Lake Mary, FL: Charisma House, 2003.

Dobson, James. *Emotions: Can You Trust Them?* Ventura, CA: Regal, 1975.

Douglass, Steve. *Enjoying Your Walk With God*. Singapore: Campus Crusade for Christ, 2001.

Edwards, Gene. *The Divine Romance*. Wheaton, IL: Tyndale, 1984.

Foster, David Kyle. *Sexual Healing*. Ventura, CA: Regal, 2005.

Frangipane, Francis. *The Three Battlegrounds*. Cedar Rapids, MI: Arrow Publications, 1989.

Guyon, Jeanne. *Experiencing the Depths of Jesus Christ*. Gardiner, ME: Christian Books, 1981.

————. *The Song of the Bride*. Sargent, GA: The SeedSowers, 1990.

Hayward, Chris. *God's Cleansing Stream*. Ventura, CA: Regal, 2004.

Hinn, Benny. *Welcome, Holy Spirit*. Nashville, TN: Thomas Nelson, 1995.

Hinn, Sam. *Kissing the Face of God*. Lake Mary, FL: Charisma House, 2002.

McClurkin, Donnie. *Eternal Victim: Eternal Victor*. Lanham, MD: Pneuma Life Publications, 2001.

MacDonald, George. *Your Life in Christ*. Minneapolis, MN: Bethany House, 2005.

McGee, Robert S. *The Search for Significance*. Houston, TX: Rapha, 1990.

Meyer, Joyce. *Help Me, I'm Depressed*. Tulsa, OK: Harrison House, 1998.

Mira, Greg. *Victim or Victor*. Grandview, MO: Grace Publishing Company, 1992.

Mouliert, Gwen. *Overcoming Bitterness*. Mansfield, PA: Winds of Fire, 2000.

Nee, Watchman. *The Release of the Spirit*. Cloverdale, IN: Ministry of Life, 1965.

Pierce, Chuck, and Rebecca Wagner Sytsema. *Possessing Your Inheritance*. Ventura, CA: Renew, 1999.

Pitts, Michael. *Help! I Think God Is Trying to Kill Me*. New Kensington, PA: Whitaker House, 2002.

Prince, Derek. *Blessing or Curse: You Can Choose*. Ann Arbor, MI: Chosen, 2000.

Rallo, Vito. *Breaking Generational Curses and Pulling Down Strongholds*. St. Louis, MO: Free Indeed Ministries, 1999.

Rodgers, Joyce. *Fatal Distractions*. Lake Mary, FL: Charisma House, 2003.

Sandford, John Loren, and Mark Sandford. *A Comprehensive Guide to Deliverance and Inner Healing*. Ann Arbor, MI: Chosen, 1992.

Scott, Kay. *Sexual Assault: Will I Ever Feel Okay Again?* Minneapolis, MN: Bethany House, 1993.

Shankle, Randy. *The Merismos.* Marshall, TX: Christian Publishing Services, Inc., 1987.

Sherrer, Quin, and Ruthanne Garlock. *A Woman's Guide to Breaking Bondages.* Ann Arbor, MI: Servant, 1994.

Sides, Dale. *Mending Cracks in the Soul.* Colorado Springs, CO: Wagner, 2002.

Smith, Alice. *Beyond the Veil.* Ventura, CA: Regal, 1997.

———. *40 Days Beyond the Veil.* Ventura, CA: Regal, 2003.

Smith, Alice, and Eddie Smith. *Spiritual Housecleaning.* Ventura, CA: Regal, 2003.

Smith, Eddie. *Breaking the Enemy's Grip.* Minneapolis, MN: Bethany House, 2004.

Wagner, Doris. *How to Minister Freedom.* Ventura, CA: Regal, 2005.

White, Paula. *He Loves Me—He Loves Me Not.* Lake Mary, FL: Charisma House, 1998.

Wilson, Ken. *How to Repair the Wrong You've Done.* Ann Arbor, MI: Servant, 1982.

Recommended Victim Resources

(1) David Kyle Foster
(Homosexuality, Lesbianism, and Sexual Dysfunctions)
Mastering Life Ministries
PO Box 351149
Jacksonville, FL 32235
904–220–7474
www.masteringlife.org

(2) Peter Horrobin
(Healing for Rejection, Loss, and Inner Pain)
2310 Leonard Drive
Seffner, FL 33584
813–657–6147
813–657–4983 (Fax)
www.usa@ellelministries.org

(3) Sherill Piscopo
Evangel Christian Churches
28491 Utica Rd.
Roseville, MI 48066
www.evangel-churches.com

(4) Chris Hayward
(Inner Healing, Abuse, Christian Growth)
Cleansing Stream Ministries
PO Box 7076
Van Nuys, CA 91409–7076
www.cleansingstream.org

(5) Kimberly Daniels
(Gangs, Deliverance, Drugs, Sexual Problems)
Spoken Word Ministries
9197 Camshire Dr.
Jacksonville, FL 32244–7425
www.kimberlydaniels.com

(6) *http://christianbest.com/xian_wom.html*
A comprehensive list of Christian organizations that help with various issues: homelessness, abuse, personal growth, single parenting, etc.

(7) *www.counselcareconnection.org*
(Anger Management)

(8) Geri McGhee
(Deliverance, Soul Ties, Strongholds)
Abiding Life Ministries
15684 C.R. 434A
Lindale, TX 75771
www.abidinglifeministries.org

(9) Jeff VanVonderen
(Spiritual Abuse)
PO Box 7481
Capistrano Beach, CA 92624
Voice: 949–677–8354;
Email: jeff@spiritualabuse.com
www.innervention.com
www.spiritualabuse.com/dox/contact.htm

(10) Vito and Pat Rallo
(Depression, Sicknesses, Strongholds)
Free Indeed Ministries
PO Box 515066
St. Louis, MO 63151–5066
www.freeindeedministries.org

(11) Eden Communications
(Sex, Love, and Relationships; also Abuse, Teens, Pornography. Site has translation into various languages.)
PO Box 200
Gilbert, AZ 85299
USA Phone: 480–507–3621
Toll free: 800–332–2261 or 888–88-BIBLE
Fax: 480–507–3623
www.christiananswers.net/love/home.html

(12) Dale Sides
(Strongholds, Healing of the Mind, Abuse, Deliverance)
Liberating Ministries for Christ, Intl.
PO Box 38
Bedford, VA 24523
540–586–5813
www.lmci.org

(13) Selwyn Stevens
(Spiritual Deception; Freemasonry, Mormonism, Watchtower, Christadelphianism, Spiritualism; New Age [including Alternative/Occultic healing therapies]; Islam, Baha'i, etc.)
Jubilee Resources, Intl.
PO Box 36–044
Wellington 6330
New Zealand
www.jubilee-resources.com

(14) Joseph Thompson
(Demonic Strongholds)
Light the Nations Ministries
PO Box 62325
Colorado Springs, CO 80962
www.lightthenations.org

(15) John and Paula Sandford
(Inner Healing, Deliverance, Rejection, Abuse)
Elijah House
17397 Laura Lane
Post Falls, ID 83854
www.elijahhouse.org

(16) Chester and Betsy Kylstra
(Curses, False Beliefs, Soul/Spirit Hurts, Demonic Oppression)
Proclaiming His Word, Inc.
Echo Mountain Inn
2849 Laurel Park Hwy.
Hendersonville, NC 28739
www.phw.org

(17) Becca Greenwood
(Strongholds, Soul Ties, Deliverance)
Christian Harvest, Intl.
http://christianharvestintl.org
Email: info@christianharvestintl.org

Endnotes

Chapter 2

1. Crume, DiGuiseppi, Byers, Sirotnak, Garrett, 2002; Herman-Giddens, Brown, Verbiest, Carlson, Hooten, et al., 1999.
2. Source: U.S. Department of Health and Human Services, Administration for Children and Families, National Clearinghouse on Child Abuse and Neglect, 2002.
3. Source: CASA Survey of Child Welfare Professionals, 1997–98.
4. FBI Uniform Crime Report, 1997.
5. *Rape in America: A Report to the Nation,* National Victim Center, 1992.
6. *Prevalence, Incidence, and Consequences of Violence Against Women,* Department of Justice, 1998.
7. Op. cit., 1992.
8. Ibid.
9. As quoted at *www.sermons.com.*

Chapter 3

1. From William Smith, L.L.D., *Bible Dictionary* (Grand Rapids, MI: Zondervan, 1948), 289.
2. All scriptural emphasis added.
3. Arthur Burk, *Overcoming the Victim Spirit* (Whittier, CA: Plumbline Ministries, 2001), 19.
4. For example, see Psalms 16:5–8; 22:9–11; 139; Isaiah 44:2.
5. For examples, see Judges 19:25; 2 Samuel 13:1–20; John 10:10.

Chapter 4

1. Brett Blair, *eSermons.com,* adapted from "First Lady" by Ann Gerhart, from *The Perfect Wife: The Life and Choices of Laura Bush,* condensed in *Reader's Digest* (January 2004).

Chapter 5

1. Arthur Gordon, *A Touch of Wonder.* Reprinted by permission of Fleming H. Revell, a division of Baker Publishing Group (Grand Rapids, MI: 1974). Quoted from Charles Swindoll, *The Tale of the Tardy Oxcart* (Nashville: Word, 1998), 583–84.
2. Adapted from Dr. Anthony T. Evans, *Guiding Your Family in a Misguided World* (Colorado Springs: Focus on the Family, 1999).

Chapter 6

1. Neil T. Anderson, *Overcoming Negative Self-Image* (Ventura, CA: Regal, 2003), 102–03.

Chapter 7

1. Gwen Mouliert, *Overcoming Bitterness: Get Away From Me, Satan!* (Mansfield, PA.: Winds of Fire, 2000), 61.
2. Dr. Bob Moorehead, *Words Aptly Spoken* (Kirkland, WA: Overlake Christian Press), 165–66.
3. Neil Anderson and Rich Miller, *Freedom From Fear* (Eugene, OR: Harvest House, 1999), 41.
4. Ibid., 259.
5. Paraphrased from online article: *en.wikipedia.org/wiki/Columbine_High_School_massacre.*
6. John Maxwell, "The Pain Principle," chapter in *Winning With*

People: Discover the People Principles That Work for You Every Time (Nashville: Nelson Business, 2005).

7. Doris Wagner, *Ministering Freedom to the Emotionally Wounded*, chapter 2, citing from Cindy Jacobs, *Releasing Bitter Root Judgments* (Colorado Springs: Wagner, 2003), 29.

8. See 1 Corinthians 15:33; Colossians 3:5; 2 Timothy 3:1–5.

9. See Proverbs 10:19–21; 12:18; Ephesians 4:31–32; Colossians 3:8.

10. See Deuteronomy 28:28–29; Proverbs 14:30; 16:24.

11. See Galatians 5:16–23.

12. See Proverbs 3:25–26; 6:10–11; 10:4; Isaiah 28:13–15.

Chapter 8

1. May 20, 2005.

2. Taken from Ken Wilson, *How to Repair the Wrong You've Done* (Grand Rapids, MI: Servant, 1982), 46.

3. Available at *www.prayerbookstore.com*.

Chapter 10

1. Copyright Integrity, Hosanna! Music, 1998.

2. Online at: *www.celebraterecovery.com/8principles.asp*. If you'd like to learn more about unforgiveness issues, I recommend my husband's book *Breaking the Enemy's Grip* (*www.prayerbookstore.com*).

3. Online at: *www.celebraterecovery.com/8principles.asp*.

Chapter 11

1. Paraphrased from account of traditional Jewish wedding, as told by Zola Levitt, Zola Levitt Ministries, Dallas.

Chapter 12

1. Adaptation of *Cinderella* from *www.pitt.edu/dash/type0510a.html.*

Testimonies

1. "He Looked Beyond My Fault and Saw My Need." Dottie Rambo, (c) 1968. John T. Benson Publishing Co., ASCAP, Administered by Brentwood-Benson Music Publishing, Inc.
2. The book contains the ten steps. *www.prayerbookstore.com*
3. Eddie Smith, *Breaking the Enemy's Grip* (Minneapolis: Bethany House, 2004).

Index

priest, 35, 41, 46, 62, 131, 143
prison, 30, 91, 157
problems, 7, 19, 23, 25, 35, 36, 38,
    39, 50, 58, 68, 74, 79, 83, 86,
    87, 113, 114, 123, 152, 153,
    161, 164, 168
proclivity, 40, 72
promiscuity, 23, 89, 169
prophetic, 147, 149
prophetic declaration, 20
psychiatrists, 11, 83, 95
psychologist, 11, 47, 111
public schools, 13, 152
Pueblo, Colorado, 166
purify, 51, 126, 139
purposes, 32, 33, 38, 48, 96, 97,
    115, 118, 122, 123, 124, 130,
    131, 133, 139

Q
qualifications, 28, 96, 132

R
racial, 30
radical, 32, 40, 93
rage, 31, 76, 82, 88, 105, 113, 114,
    115, 118, 162
Rambo, Dottie, 169
rape, 21, 22, 46, 49, 125, 154, 162
Rape in America, 22
real estate, 69
rebellion, 41, 44, 71, 154, 159, 160
redirection, 82
rejection, 18, 25, 31, 32, 50, 51,
    64, 66, 116, 117, 139, 142,
    143
release, 87, 92, 96, 100, 118, 123,
    142, 159
religious spirit, 76, 89
renters, 69
reoccurrences, 98
repression, 84
resent, 84, 88, 92, 114, 123, 142

respect, 23, 43, 106, 118, 122, 124,
    128
responders, 120
restoring, 29, 120
retarded, 30
Ricky, 26, 27
righteousness, 29, 62, 73, 114, 119,
    121, 124, 129, 133, 143, 149
Roe, Ted, 147, 149
Ron and Betty, 27
Ronnie, 31, 32, 33
root, 32, 41, 50, 63, 72, 77, 86, 87,
    92, 93, 96, 101, 102, 103,
    122, 126
root of bitterness, 88
rowdy, 26
royalty, 150

S
sabotage, 27
salvation, 59, 60, 74, 102, 124,
    139, 143, 157
Sarah, 65, 66
Satan, 11, 29, 64, 65, 83, 96, 97,
    119, 129, 130, 135, 157, 159,
    161, 170
Satanism, 82, 94, 95
Saturday Night Live, 11
savings, 27
scars, 15
scholarship, 25
school, 17, 18, 24, 25, 26, 31, 32,
    47, 84, 85, 152, 154, 156,
    162, 165
Scott, Sir Walter, 30
screaming, 16, 17, 36, 119
secret, 15, 76, 97, 126, 137, 143,
    148, 169
sects, 55, 81, 89
self-condemnation, 40
self-mutilation, 82
self-pity, 41
senior pastor, 28